SIGNS FOR ALL SEASONS

MORE SIGN LANGUAGE GAMES

BY: SUZIE LINTON KIRCHNER

First Printing.................November 1977
Second Printing................December 1978
Third Printing.................June 1979
Fourth Printing................February 1981

ISBN NUMBER 0-917002-19-9

Library of Congress Number: 77-93546

Illustrated by Frank Allen Paul
Layout by Stephanie Pyren

For· information concerning this publication please contact:

JOYCE MEDIA, INC.
8753 Shirley Avenue
PO Box 458
Northridge, California 91328
Telephone (213) 885-7181 - Voice or TTY

DEDICATED TO:

"GRAMMY"

who is a woman for all seasons

· Index ·

FINGERSPELLING, SIGN, GESTURE OR PANTOMIME

SIGN GAMES

NUMBER and/or FINGERSPELLING GAMES

GESTURE OR PANTOMIME, EXPRESSION OR MOVEMENT

Special Thanks To

Carl, for his love and encouragement to continue this project.

CJ, JonE, Jenny and Maje who were the first field testers for many of these games.

Frank Allen Paul for making each game come to life!

John Joyce for getting involved "the second time around!"

Dee Walker for the arduous initial typing.

FOREWORD:

For the serious teacher of manual communication, the struggle to find exciting ways of acquiring and reinforcing vocabulary and developing in the students a sense of comfort with a new means of communication is a never-ending challenge. The present volume, coupled with Mrs. Kirchner's earlier work Play It By Sign serves as an invaluable collection of activities which, if used properly, can make the learning task exciting and fun for both student and teacher. The range of activities described in this volume not only span the spectrum of signing skills (beginning through advanced) but also provide sufficient variety to challenge and excite any class.

Perhaps the greatest value of this volume lies in the fact that it provides ready-made opportunities which allow the students to participate in meaningful communication situations. It is only when a person experiences a feeling of success in using a language or mode of communication that he or she truly begins to learn that language or communication mode. The activities and games included herein will provide such experiences in gestures, mime, signs and fingerspelling. Additionally, there are ample activities which can serve to develop readiness skills, imitation, visual perception, etc. - which are vital to any success with manual communication.

The concise, clear explanation of activities, the inclusion of comprehensive word lists, poems and item lists and the "Copy Me" pages insure a minimum of teacher preparation time. This book is a welcome complement to Play It By Sign in the library of students and teachers of manual communication.

Dennis Cokely

Communications Specialist-Sign Language
Kendall Demonstration Elementary School
Gallaudet College
Wshington, D.C.

Introduction and Instructions

Signs For All Seasons, like its predecessor, Play It By Sign (Joyce Media, Inc. 1974) contains games and activities to be played in pantomime, gestures, fingerspelling and sign language. These games and activities can be used for initial teaching, as reinforcement for previously learned material, or just for fun. They are meant not only for hearing impaired children and adults but also for others with normal hearing whose minds are language locked, rather than their ears.

This book is specifically recommended for:

1. Classes of adults or children learning manual communication.

2. Classes of deaf children where Total Communication is employed.

3. Classes of language and/or speech handicapped children (autistic, aphasic, brain damaged, mentally retarded) where manual communication is used to facilitate and free communication.

4. Classes of physically handicapped children where manual communication could be used for additional practice in motor control.

5. Classes of "normal" children to provide exposure and under- standing of language in a different modality.

6. Homes in which there are deaf children with hearing parents or hearing children with deaf parents.

7. Social gatherings of deaf and/or hearing people just for fun!

Feedback from Play It By Sign indicates that users also found it beneficial for teaching lipreading, speech and listening skills. Its companion, Signs For All Seasons should also prove helpful in these areas.

Each game or activity is written in a simple step by step format. A
quick glance at the top of each game will tell you:

I.   The <u>Objective</u> of the specific game (what you are trying to
        accomplish.)

II.   The <u>Value</u>-how it will help your students.

III.   The <u>Level</u>-beginning, intermediate or advanced level in
        manual communication class. Also indicated is the approximate
        age groups for which it is best suited.

IV.   The <u>Mode</u> of performance-pantomime, gesture, fingerspelling
        or <u>signs</u>.

V.   The <u>Materials Needed</u>-what to buy (if necessary), or how to
        make <u>it</u>.

VI.   <u>How to Play</u>-how to arrange the players, play and score the
        game (if desired) and ways to vary it and/or increase the level
        of difficulty.

Throughout the book appendices appear immediately after certain games.
These appendices are divided into three catagories:

1.   Pages that the teacher may duplicate for student use. These
        pages are marked "Copy Me".

2.   Pages of information to be transferred to 3X5 cards, etc.
        These pages may NOT be duplicated.

3.   Pages with lists of words that the teacher may remove from
        the book and hold easily while playing the game. These
        pages may NOT be duplicated.

Note: The games and any other portion of the book that is not marked
        COPY ME, may NOT be duplicated in any manner as it is protected
        under copyright.

There are three ways to duplicate the COPY ME pages. The method you choose
will depend on the hardware that is available to you. Remove the
needed sheet from the binder and:

Method 1.   Make the needed number of copies on a Xerox, Apeco Super
              Start or similar copying machine.

Method 2.   a. Make one (thermal) ditto master on a 3M "96" or
                  similar machine.

              b. Use this ditto master to run the number of copies
                  needed (purple ink).

Method 3.   a. Make one stencil master on a Gestetner Stencil Maker or
                  similar machine.

              b. Use this stencil on a mimeograph machine to make the
                  number of copies needed (black ink).

This book is available in two forms-perfect bound and in a ring binder.
The ring binder form is so that pages may be easily removed to teach
from or copy and so that you may add your own 8½X11 sheets with notes,
additional ideas etc.
One item that I suggested to users of the first book has proved to be
very valuable. That is the purchase of a clear page protector,
punched for ring binder. This allows the teacher to remove a
game, place it in the page protector and carry it in a lesson plan
book or other book without having to carry the entire Signs For
All Seasons ring binder to class.
These games can be played using manual communication regardless of the
specific orientation. Most are suitable for Ameslan (American Sign
Language), S.E.E. or any form of Siglish (Signed English). The use
or non-use of lip movement or voice with the adult student will depend
on the individual teacher's background, philosophy and purpose. I
personally play these games without lip movement or voice as I want
the adult student to read signs and not lips. However for other
activities with my class period, lip movement and sometimes speech is
used in order to teach coordination of speech and sign and instill
an even rhythm and natural flow. Usually when playing most of these
games in the educational setting with children, SPEECH with AMPLIFICATION
is used in conjunction with sign language.
The use of class members as leaders in some of these games is especially
valuable as it provides the teacher a chance to see the students in action
and also gives other students a chance to read hands other than the
teacher's.
I hope that the wide variety of games and activities within these pages
will provide each teacher with ideas and ways to make every lesson in
sign language more interesting and meaningful. I hope also that you
will find activites which allow you to build on, or remediate existing
skills. The scope of this volume truly makes it a book of Signs for
All Seasons.

                        "Signed",
                        Suzie Linton Kirchner

NOTES

FINGERSPELLING
GAMES

I. OBJECTIVE: To build words in crossword puzzle fashion.

II. VALUE: To increase recognition of fingerspelling through the printed form.

III. LEVEL: Adults - Beginning through advanced.
Children - 8 years old and up.

IV. MODE: Fingerspelling in printed form.

V. MATERIALS NEEDED:

1. Playing board(s) (see Appendix).

2. 140 letter squares (ses Appendix).

a. letter distribution and values

LETTER	DISTRIBUTION	VALUE
A	10	1
B	4	6
C	4	6
D	6	2
E	14	1
F	3	8
G	4	6
H	5	4
I	10	1
J	2	10
K	2	10
L	6	2
M	4	6
N	8	2
O	10	1
P	3	8
Q	2	10
R	8	2
S	6	2
T	10	1
U	6	2
V	3	8
W	3	8
X	1	12
Y	4	6
Z	2	10

3. Letter holders (**one** per player). (See Illustration)

4. Pencil and paper to keep score.

To assemble 1 - 2 - 3.

    a. Make copies of letter squares as needed (one set per game board). Then cut out letter squares on solid lines.

    b. Fold paper to make letter holder as illustrated.

    c. Make copies of the board as needed. Then mount on cardboard or tag board and laminate both sides for durability (or cover with clear contact paper).

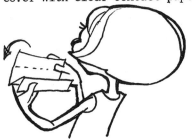

FOLDED LETTER HOLDER
(any paper will do)

VI. TO PLAY: (2-6 players)

1. Mix letter squares face down in a box lid or similar device.

2. Each player draws 9 letter squares and places them on the holder.

3. Place playing board in center of players.

4. Each player adds up the values on his 9 letter squares. The player with the highest total plays first. Play then passes to the left. (If there is a tie then the two players redraw 9 new letter squares).

5. Choose one person to keep score.

6. The first player places 2 or more letter squares that form a word so that part of it touches on the "I love you" sign in the center of the playing board.

7. The second player then creates another word by adding his letters to that of the first player either horizontally or vertically. (<u>not</u> diagonally)

8. Play continues in like manner with each player forming a new word on some previously made word.

9. As each player uses some of his letter squares in his turn, he then replaces them by drawing the same number of new letter squares from the box lid, so that his holder always has 9 letter squares.

10. Play continues until the box lid is empty and all possible plays are exhausted.

The Rules of Dactabble.

1. Words may be any found in the dictionary except proper names, foreign words, hyphenated words and abbreviations.

2. Add 15 points to the total word score if the word covers a "Suzie Sign" block.

3. Individual letters that are placed on blocks containing numbers are increased by that number.

   e.g. a <u>J</u> that is worth <u>10</u> and is placed on a <u>6</u> then equals <u>16</u>.

4. When 2 or more words are formed in one turn then each is counted separately.

5. Words may be repeated.

6. To score a word add up the value of each letter, including that of special blocks that may have been covered. Tell the total to the scorekeeper who records it.

7. The winner is the player with the highest score.

<u>NOTE</u>: All conversation among players including delivery of scores is strictly by sign or fingerspelling.

VARIATION I:

   I. <u>OBJECTIVE</u>: To build words in crossword puzzle fashion by covering the <u>printed</u> words on the board with the corresponding finger-spelling letter squares.

  II. <u>VALUE</u>:

   1. To teach or reinforce the correspondence between the printed letter and the fingerspelled letter.

   2. To teach children to work crossword puzzles.

   3. Enjoyment.

 III. <u>LEVEL</u>: Beginning through advanced. (Young children)

  IV. <u>MODE</u>: Fingerspelling.

   V. <u>MATERIALS</u> <u>NEEDED</u>:

   1. All items for basic game.

   2. <u>Unmounted</u> and <u>unlaminated</u> playing board(s) with selected words printed <u>on</u> the board(s) (one letter per block).

VI. TO PLAY:

1. Teacher prints selected words on the board in crossword style with a pen. Choose words to be taught, reinforced or reviewed.

2. Each child chooses five letter squares.

3. Choose one child to be first.

4. That child finds any two letters on the board for which he has the corresponding fingerspelling squares and places them on the letters.

5. He then chooses two more squares from the box lid to replace the two used.

6. Play passes to the player on the left who places 2 of his squares just as the first player has done. He draws two replacement squares.

7. Play continues in like manner.

8. When a child covers the last letter of a word, then that word is his. The scorekeeper writes that word under the child's name.

9. The winner is the child with the most words.

VARIATION II:

1. As above only use the board from SCRABBLE for Juniors (Selchow and Righter Co.). The yellow side is the easiest one and the blue side more advanced for children who can spell well.

2. Use rules of DACTABBLE or of SCRABBLE for Juniors but use the fingerspelling squares rather than the letter tiles.

6

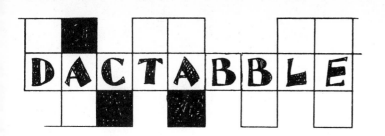

DACTABBLE

COPY·ME

	5			8		6
	3	7			4	
		1		2		
10						9
9						10
	2		1			
4		7		3		
6		8			5	

7

1 1 1 1 1 1 1 1 1 6 6 6 6
6 6 6 6 2 2 2 2 2 2 1 1 1 1
1 1 1 1 1 1 1 1 1 1 8 8 8 6
6 6 6 4 4 4 4 4 1 1 1 1 1 1
1 1 1 1 10 10 10 10 2 2 2 2 2 2
6 6 6 6 2 2 2 2 2 2 2 2 1 1
1 1 1 1 1 1 1 1 8 8 8 10 10 2
2 2 2 2 2 2 2 2 2 2 2 2 2 1
1 1 1 1 1 1 1 1 2 2 2 2 2
2 8 8 8 8 8 8 12 6 6 6 6 10 10

DACTYL DECK

I.   OBJECTIVE: To match the pictures of the fingerspelled letter with the
     correct letter in print.

II. VALUE: To show the relationship of fingerspelling to letters in the
     printed form.

III. LEVEL: Beginning adults or young children.

IV. MODE: Fingerspelling in the printed form.

V.   MATERIALS NEEDED:

     1. One Dactyl Deck. (52 cards). (See Appendix)

VI. TO PLAY: Game A (2 players)

     1. Shuffle the cards and deal out evenly between 2 players A and B.

     2. Players hold stacks face down.

     3. Player A turns up his top card. Player B turns up his top card.
         If it is a match then "A" takes both cards.

     4. Player B now turns up his next card, and player A follows. If it
         is a match then "B" takes both cards.

NOTE: If there is no match then each player takes back his card and places it
       on the bottom of his stack.

     5. The player with the most matched pairs wins the game.

             Game B (2-4 players)

     1. Shuffle the cards and deal out evenly among the players.

     2. Each player removes the matched pairs and places them face down
         in front of him.

     3. The first player spreads his cards in a fan and the player on
         his left draws one. If it makes a pair then it is placed face
         down. If it does not, the card is added to the hand.

     4. Play continues in like manner with the player offering his cards
         to the one on his left. As matches are made they are placed
         face down.

5. The winner is the player with the most matched pairs.

Game C (simple activity for 1 person)

1. Lay out either the fingerspelled cards or the letter cards on a table. Then match the other set to it.

Game D (2 to 4 players - rules are like "Fish")

1. Deal out five cards per player. Put remaining cards in the center.

2. Player to the left of dealer begins by laying down any matched pairs in his hand. Then he can ask any player for a card he needs by fingerspelling that letter.

3. If the person requested has that letter he must give them to the requester. If he does not have it, the requester picks up a card from the center pile.

4. Play continues in like manner until all the cards are matched.

5. Player with the most matched pairs wins.

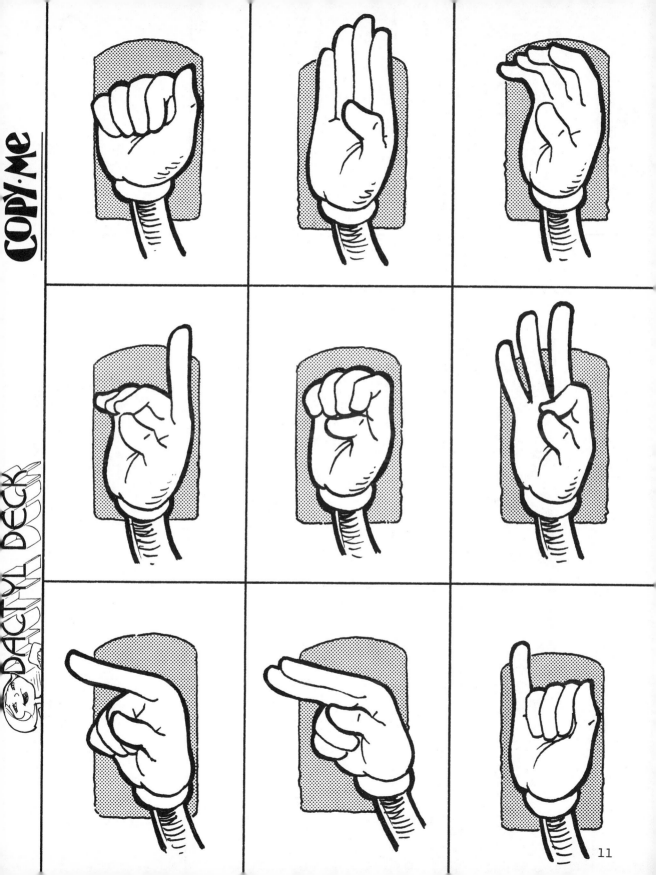

DACTYL DECK

13

Aa Bb Cc

Dd Ee Ff

Gg Hh Ii

J j K k L l

M m N n O o

P p Q q R r

S s	T t	U u
V v	W w	X x
Y y	Z z	

DACTYL DECK

16

I.   OBJECTIVE: To add a letter to an already started sequence of letters without finishing the word.

II. VALUE: 1. To increase memory for fingerspelled letters.
             2. To help recall the actual spelling of words in everyday use.
             3. To sharpen perception of misspelled words or sequences of letters that are not real words.

III. LEVEL: Beginning through advanced. (Upper elementary grades to adult)

IV. MODE: Fingerspelling.

V.   MATERIALS NEEDED:

     1. Thinking caps.

VI. TO PLAY:

     1. Divide the players into two teams.

     2. The first player on Team A fingerspells one letter.

     3. The next player adds a letter but he must have a word in mind.

     4. The play continues with each player adding a letter, thus spelling out a word.

     5. If at anytime a player adds a letter and the opposing team thinks it is not a real word, they may say "We doubt it." If the player can spell a real word, his team gets a point. If he can't, the opposing team gets the point.

     6. If a player adds a letter that finishes a word, the opposing team gets a point.

hinky-pinky

I. OBJECTIVE: To guess the phrase from a given definition.

II. VALUE: To increase the ability to read short groups of words in finger-spelling and to have fun with words.

III. LEVEL: Intermediate to advanced. (Junior high school to adult)

IV. MODE: Fingerspelling.

V. MATERIALS NEEDED:

    1. Thinking caps.

    2. Appendix A or B.

VI. TO PLAY:

    1. Teacher chooses definition-phrase sets from the Appendix and fingerspells the definitions (Column A) one at a time to the students.

    2. Players volunteer with the correct phrases. (Column B).

NOTE: This activity requires some agility with words. To make the activity one of reception only, minus mental agility, use the following variation.

VARIATION I:

    1. Choose some definition-phrase sets.

    2. Write the phrases (Column B) in random order on the board or mimeographed on paper for distribution to players.

    3. Fingerspell the definitions (Column A) one at a time.

    4. Players peruse the list of phrases and if they understood the definition they will quickly find the corresponding phrases.

APPENDIX: A - HINKY-PINKY

COLUMN A	COLUMN B
DEFINITIONS	PHRASES
cinder serving piece (=)	ash tray
large swine	big pig
drenched dog	wet pet
short sorrow	brief grief
pertrified fossil	stone bone
indigo church bench	blue pew
obese feline	fat cat
unlighted playground	dark park
deceased Frederick	dead Fred
rosy basin	pink sink
ironed jerkin	pressed vest
highest quality nuisance	best pest
solitary fencepost	sole pole
fake colt	phoney pony
tatter combustion	higher fire
glass gun	crystal pistol
fur furniture	hair chair
more stern tombstone	starker marker
jaunty Thanksgiving bird	jerkey turkey
higher quality cardigan	better sweater
ridiculous flower	silly lily
cantaloupe thief	melon felon
whale washer	blubber scrubber
thicker serving plate	fatter platter
blazing hedge	burning bush
twirling tire	spinning wheel
infant mug	baby face
5,280 ft pebble	mile stone
flabby meow	fat cat
pooped corpuscles	tired blood
not a puff in the heavens	not a cloud in the sky
final yet not littlest	last but not least
vanished with the blowhard	gone with the wind
elevate five fingers	raise your hand
tuneful stools	musical chairs
postage saver	stamp collector
as chilly as an unpickled pickle	cool as a cucumber

APPENDIX: B   HINKY-PINKY

COLUMN A	COLUMN B
DEFINITIONS	PHRASES
in the attic + in the cellar	upstairs, downstairs
puckers up + spills the beans	kiss and tell
Isabella's hubby + cow's hubby	Ferdinand the Bull
Mr. Burns + Tom Sawyer's boat	George Raft
bottle top + evening dress	cap and gown
60 seconds + box step	minute waltz
lock opener + cavity	key hole
toss + carpet	throw rug
navel + ballerina	belly dancer
24 gauge + "I do"	shotgun wedding
celestial + zebra skin	stars and stripes
jackass + caboose	mule train
boot + bugle	shoe horn
not easy + derby	hard hat
on the cob + snowdrop	cornflakes
gardenia + gal	flower girl
beantown + daddys	Boston pops
scribble + brethren	Wright Brothers

I. OBJECTIVE: To arrange the cubes to make as many words as possible horizontally and vertically.

II. VALUE: To give practice in reading fingerspelling from the players hands and also to read the graphic representation of the manual alphabet.

III. LEVEL: Beginning through advanced. (Upper elementary to advanced)

IV. MODE: Fingerspelling.

V. MATERIALS NEEDED:

   1. One game of KEEP QUIET The Sign Language Crosswood Cubes Game published by

      Kopptronix Co.   (Pat. Pend.)
      Stanhope, NJ 07874

VI. TO PLAY:

   1. Follow directions in booklet for exact playing directions.

VARIATIONS I & II:

   Included in the booklet.

I.   OBJECTIVE: To make words that contain the given letter pattern by
     matching the definition.

II. VALUE: To increase the ability to read <u>whole letter patterns</u> in finger-
     spelling.

III. LEVEL: Beginning through advanced. (Junior high school to adults)

IV. MODE: Fingerspelling.

V.   MATERIALS NEEDED:

     1. Appendix.

     2. Thinking caps.

VI. TO PLAY: METHOD A - (one large group)

     1. Teacher or student teacher fingerspells a letter pattern to the
         group.

     2. Next, definitions are signed or fingerspelled one at a time and
         class members take turns fingerspelling new words that match
         the definitions and contain the given letter pattern.

         METHOD B - (several small groups)

     1. Play as in METHOD A except there are several small groups and
         one "teacher" for each. Teachers may be given the same lists of
         words so each group is working on the same words, or the large
         list (Appendix)   may be divided among the groups.

APPENDIX: PATTERNS PLUS

PATTERN	DEFINITION	WORD
	connection	link
	kind of fur	mink
INK	pale red	pink
	a place to skate	rink
	a place to wash	sink
	a seat	chair
	honest	fair
AIR	skin covering	hair
	lion's den	lair
	two of a kind	pair
	season	fall
	high	tall
ALL	round toy	ball
	gust of wind	squall
	corridor	hall
	opposite of front	back
	to break	crack
ACK	small quick repast	snack
	to pile	stack
	absence or shortage	lack
	to create	made
	sun shield	shade
ADE	lose color	fade
	part of knife	blade
	difficulty in moving	wade
	links	chain
	to empty	drain
AIN	small particle	grain
	hurt	pain
	precipitation	rain
	naked	bare
	attention	care
ARE	flame	flare
	stare	glare
	fruit	pear
	wooden box	crate
	palm fruit	date
ATE	destiny	fate
	grind	grate
	tardy	late

APPENDIX: PATTERNS PLUS

	truthful	honest
	coins, dollars	money
ONE	single	alone
	king's seat	throne
	skeleton part	bone
	gentile woman	lady
	part of knife	blade
LAD	used to climb	ladder
	part of meal	salad
	user for gravy	ladle
	female	woman
	to order	command
MAN	lion hair	mane
	living person	human
	proper actions	manners

APPENDIX: PATTERNS PLUS (Continued)

PATTERN	DEFINITION	WORD
	earth mixture	clay
	not night	day
AY	ravel	fray
	a drama	play
	beam	ray
	overcome	beat
	lamb cry	bleat
EAT	defraud	cheat
	deed	feat
	a pleasure	treat
	past of blow	blew
	beer preparation	brew
EW	gang	crew
	past of pull	drew
	past of flourish	grew
	to grade	mark
	sea related	marine
MAR	language rules	grammar
	parade	march
	store	market
	brave	bold
	not hot	cold
OLD	precious metal	gold
	related	told
	rebuke	scold

APPENDIX: PATTERNS PLUS (Continued)

PATTERN	DEFINITION	WORD
RAT	grind	grate
	to create power	generate
	anger	wrath
	to run	operate
	baby toy	rattle
RAN	wonderful	grand
	change places	transfer
	piece of rope	strand
	stove	range
	to rate	rank
HER	not any place	nowhere
	distant place	there
	plume	feather
	famous person	hero
	animal group	herd
DEN	car crash	accident
	thick	dense
	unexpected	sudden
	a recess	indentation
	concerning teeth	dental
PEN	rely on	depend
	opposite of closed	open
	pay out money	spend
	waiting	pending
	to make deeper	deepen
EER	malt beverage	beer
	mirth	cheer
	horned animal	deer
	sly look	leer
	strange	queer
ENT	not straight	bent
	penny	cent
	depression	dent
	not borrowed	lent
	payment	rent
ITE	portion	bite
	summon	cite
	small amount	mite
	positively	quite
	malice	spite

APPENDIX:

PATTERN	DEFINITION	WORD
	uninteresting	bore
	apple center	core
ORE	in front	fore
	folk tales	lore
	hurting	sore
	to move air	blow
	blackbird	crow
OW	circulate liquid	flow
	flourish	grow
	recognize	know
	past of buy	bought
	past of fight	fought
OUGHT	nothing	nought
	attempted	sought
	imagined	thought
	a failure	bust
	outer shell	crust
UST	dry particles	dust
	desire	lust
	ferric oxide	rust
	conjunction	but
	sever	cut
UT	stamina	gut
	protrude	jut
	dry seed	nut
	pal	chum
	percussive	drum
UM	sad	glum
	purple fruit	plum
	stagnant liquid	scum
	to redden	blush
	compress	crush
USH	soft long pile	plush
	hurry	rush
	watery snow	slush
	distribute	dole
	cavity	hole
OLE	burrowing animal	mole
	long slender wood	pole
	only	sole

RHYME & REASON

I. <u>OBJECTIVE</u>: To find a word that rhymes with the last word in line one and matches the definition in line two of each couplet.

II. <u>VALUE</u>: To increase receptive fingerspelling ability for short phrases when part of the phrase remains constant.

III. <u>LEVEL</u>: Beginning through advanced. (Upper elementary to adult)

IV. <u>MODE</u>: Fingerspelling.

V. <u>MATERIALS NEEDED</u>:

    1. Appendix.

    2. Thinking caps.

VI. <u>TO PLAY</u>:

    1. Teacher or student teacher fingerspells a couplet from Appendix.

    2. Students are chosen or volunteer to fill in the missing word.

APPENDIX: - RHYME AND REASON

It rhymes with <u>task</u>. Means to question or to ___. (ask)

It rhymes with <u>fun</u>. A weapon called a ___. (gun)

It rhymes with <u>jog</u>. A piece of wood called a ___. (log)

It rhymes with <u>boy</u>. It's happiness or ___. (joy)

It rhymes with <u>seam</u>. The top on milk or ____. (cream)

It rhymes with <u>ink</u>. To concentrate or ____. (think)

It rhymes with <u>drive</u>. A number named ___. (five)

It rhymes with <u>true</u>. A lovely color called ___. (blue)

It rhymes with <u>four</u>. An opening called a ___. (door)

It rhymes with <u>gate</u>. A tropical fruit called ___. (date)

NOTE: Teacher can use rhyming words in dictionary to create dozens of couplets like these examples.

UPSTAIRS DOWNSTAIRS

I. OBJECTIVE: To fill in the blanks with the appropriate words.

II. VALUE: To provide an interesting way to evaluate fingerspelling reception.

III. LEVEL: Beginning through advanced. (Upper elementary to adult)

IV. MODE: Fingerspelling.

V. MATERIALS NEEDED:

1. Sufficient copies of the "Copy Me" page for the members of the class.

2. Thinking caps.

VI. TO PLAY:

1. Choose 26 words, each starting with a different letter of the alphabet.

2. Have teacher or class member fingerspell the words (either in alphabetical order or in random order) one at a time.

3. Class members fill in the steps by writing in the fingerspelled words on the appropriate line.

4. The game is completed when all the steps are filled.

NOTE: This activity provides clues as to beginning letters if done in alphabetical order. If done in random order, each step successfully filled in, narrows the possibilities and forces the reader to make educated guesses, even if they don't catch every letter on the hand.

UPSTAIRS
DOWNSTAIRS

COPY ME

32

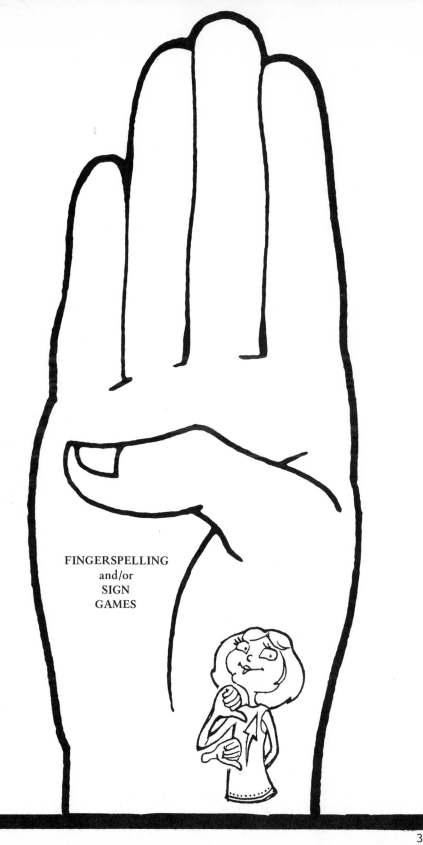

FINGERSPELLING
and/or
SIGN
GAMES

AUNTIE ANTONYM

COPY-ME

I.   OBJECTIVE: To collect as many matched pairs as possible and not be caught holding Auntie Antonym.

II. VALUE: To provide practice in the signs for English antonyms or in fingerspelling.

III. LEVEL: Beginning and intermediate. (Children to adults)

IV. MODE: Signs or fingerspelling.

V.   MATERIALS NEEDED:

    1. Blank playing cards or 6x8 index cards cut in half, (as many as desired).

    2. Words from the Appendix.

    3. One Auntie Antonym card.

    4. Roget's Thesaurus for additional antonyms.

VI. TO PLAY:

    1. Using word pairs from the Appendix write one word per card.

    2. Xerox a copy of Auntie Antonym. Cut it out and paste it on one card.

    3. Prepare 20 to 30 cards for one deck plus one Auntie Antonym card.

    4. Deal five (5) cards per player (2-4 players per game).

    5. Put the remaining cards face down on the table. They are Auntie's House.

    6. The player on the left of the dealer lays down any pairs in his hand and then asks any other player for a card he needs.

    Beginners might sign or fingerspell set phrases i.e.:

May I have _____ ?	I need _____ ?
Do you have _____ ?	I want _____ ?

7. The other player must give up the card if he has it. If he does not have it he tells the player (in sign or fingerspelling) "Go to Auntie's House" (pick a card from the center pile) or if he has the Auntie Antonym card in his hand he may quietly give that to the player instead as if it were the requested card.

8. Play continues in like manner until all the cards are used up and all the pairs are made.

9. The person with the greatest number of pairs is the winner and the person left with Auntie Antonym becomes the one to deal the next hand or lead the next activity or whatever "prize" the teacher can devise for holding that dubious distinction!

VARIATION I: (a reading only game for elementary age children)

1. Play the game using the rules of Old Maid.

VARIATION II:

1. Use as a simple drill (without the cards) for reading signs or fingerspelling.

APPENDIX: AUNTIE ANTONYM

Copy one word per card. Every card in deck must have a match.

hot - cold
soft - hard
big - little
fast - slow
high - low
black - white
up - down
over - under
in - out
always - never
happy - sad
loose - tight
tall - short
fat - thin
wide - narrow
live - die
on - off
even - odd
straight - crooked
bright - dull

intelligent - stupid
dark - light
light - heavy
give - take
come - go
quiet - noisy
deaf - hearing
strong - weak
sweet - sour
poor - rich
full - empty
(sit - stand)
(run - walk)
boy - girl
love - hate
short - long
warm - cool
open - closed (shut)
near - far
straight - bent (curved)

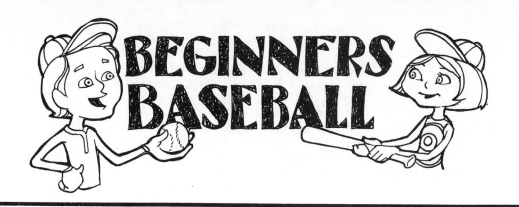

BEGINNERS BASEBALL

I. OBJECTIVE: To recognize individual signs and fingerspell their referents - or the reverse process.

II. VALUE: To provide practice in instant recognition of signs and fingerspelled words.

III. LEVEL: Beginning. (Pre-school through primary grades)

IV. MODE: Any two of the following:

    1. Pictures or real objects.

    2. Signs

    3. Fingerspelling

V. MATERIALS NEEDED:

    1. Lists of words for which signs have been previously taught, or

    2. Pictures of objects for which signs have been previously taught. (If playing with young children)

VI. TO PLAY:

    1. Divide the players into two equal teams.

    2. Make a baseball diamond on the floor using books, chairs, beanbags or teacher devised items as bases.

    3. Choose a pitcher for each team.

    4. Teacher or other student teacher must act as umpire and scorekeeper.

    5. Pitcher A gives the picture, sign or fingerspelled word to the first batter on Team B. (See Variations). If the batter answers correctly he gets a "single" and goes to first base. If he misses it is an "out".

6. Game continues with players moving from first to second to third to home as batters answer correctly. Each "batter" who misses makes an "out". Three "outs" and the other team comes to bat.

7. To score: each player who progresses around the bases and finally reaches home, scores a run for his team. The team with the highest number of "runs", after a predetermined number of innings, are played is the winner.

VARIATIONS   (Choose one)

Pitcher gives	Batter gives
an object	the sign
a picture	the sign
an object	the fingerspelled word
a picture	the fingerspelled word
a fingerspelled word	the sign
the sign	the fingerspelled word

THE GO TOGETHER GAME

I.   OBJECTIVE: To make pairs of items that naturally go together.

II. VALUE: To build expressive and receptive vocabulary using everyday familiar items.

III. LEVEL: Beginning through advanced. (Upper elementary to adult)

IV. MODE: Signs or fingerspelling.

V.   MATERIALS NEEDED:

   1. Appendix.

   2. Thinking caps.

VI. TO PLAY:

   1. Teacher or student teacher signs or fingerspells the given word of a pair in the Appendix plus the word "AND".

   2. Students respond by giving the word that goes with the given word. Eg. bread and butter.

APPENDIX: - THE GO TOGETHER GAME

Given word	Response
shoes (and)	stockings (socks)
needle	thread
bread	butter (water)
horse	wagon (carriage) (cart)
table	chair
cup	saucer
bacon	eggs
cheese	crackers
peaches	cream
love	marriage
pad	pencil
pen	ink
neat	clean
ice cream	cake
wine	roses (cheese)
sweet	sour
boys	girls
bow	arrow
hammer	nail

APPENDIX:

Given word	Response	Given Word	Response
buttons (and)	bows	king (and)	queen
soup	sandwiches (nuts)	knife	fork
toast	jelly	fork	spoon
peanut butter	jelly	down	out (under)
dollars	cents	song	dance
cats	dogs	rock	roll (Rye)
hot	dry	surf	sand (turf)
pots	pans	doctor	nurse
cold	damp	coat	tie
purse	gloves	black tie	tails
hat	coat	ball	chain (socket)
sugar	cream (spice)	rhyme	reason
cowboys	Indians	law	order
chip	dip	Amos	Andy
fish	chips	Beauty	(the) Beast
bat	ball	silk	satin
lettuce	tomato	cloak	dagger
washer	dryer		
pizza	beer		
husband	wife		
brother	sister		
aunt	uncle		
niece	nephew		
Laurel	Hardy		
Abbott	Costello		
Batman	Robin		
Chip	Dale		
ham	cheese		
salt	pepper		
Martin	Lewis		
Sears	Roebuck		
Huntley	Brinkley		
P's	Q's		
question	answer		
sun	moon		
son	daughter		
friends	lovers (relatives)		
meat	potatoes		
turkey	stuffing (dressing)		
pins	needles		
(an) arm	(a leg)		
arm(s)	leg(s)		
Arm	Hammer		
cops	robbers		
Army	Navy		
Democrat	Republican		
silver	gold		
bride	groom		
body	soul		

GO TO THE HEAD OF THE CLASS

I. <u>OBJECTIVE</u>: To move from the first desk in Kindergarten on the playing board to the last desk in Grade 8 by correctly answering questions.

II. <u>VALUE</u>: To provide opportunity for using and reading Manually Coded English (MCE).

III. <u>LEVEL</u>: Intermediate through advanced. (Junior high school to adults)

IV. <u>MODE</u>: Finderspelling and/or signs

V. <u>MATERIALS</u>:

1. One or more copies of the game called: <u>Go to the Head of the Class</u>. (Published and copyrighted in 1967 by Milton Bradley, Springfield, MA.)

VI. <u>TO PLAY</u>: (2-9 players)

Follow the instructions included in the game, translating all the questions into one of the forms of Manually Coded English, without using voice.

HOMONYMS HOMOPHENES

I. <u>OBJECTIVE</u>: To supply a word that is homonymous with a given word.
(See NOTE that proceeds Appendix).

II. <u>VALUE</u>: To increase visual perception for fingerspelling and to become
aware of words that sound <u>alike</u> in preparation for the <u>auditory</u>
decoding of words in interpreting situations.

III. <u>LEVEL</u>: Beginning through advanced. (Junior high school to adults)

IV. <u>MODE</u>: Signs and/or fingerspelling.

V. <u>MATERIALS NEEDED</u>:

    1. Appendix.

    2. Thinking caps.

    3. Blank playing cards or 6x8 index cards cut in half (for Variation II).

VI. <u>TO PLAY</u>: METHOD A (1 group)

    1. Teacher or student teacher gives a word from Column A (or B) by
signing or fingerspelling it with mouthing but <u>no</u> voice.

    2. Teacher chooses or a student volunteers to give the homonymous
word from Column B (or A).

        METHOD B (several small groups)

    1. Same as for METHOD A except there are several small groups, each
with a teacher.

        METHOD C (team play)

    1. Divide the group into 2 teams.

    2. Choose one person to be the teacher.

    3. Choose one person to be the scorekeeper.

    4. Teacher using list from Appendix A signs or fingerspells as in
METHOD A one word from Column A (or B) and first person on Team
A gives the homonymous word from Columns B (or A).

5. Teacher continues as above going from Team A to Team B down the line.

6. Team members who miss go to the end of the line instead of sitting out so they have continued changes for success.

7. Scorekeeper should keep record either of words missed or words successfully matched, whichever is easier.

8. Team with the least number of misses is the winner.

VARIATION I:

1. Teacher fingerspells a word from Column A (or B) and the student uses its homonym from Column B (or A) in a short sentence.

VARIATION II:

1. Using word pairs from the Appendix, write one word per card.

2. Prepare 30 to 40 cards for one deck.

3. Shuffle and deal out five (5) cards per player (2-4 players a game).

4. Put the remaining cards face down on the table. They are "Hubby Homonym's Hangout".

5. The player on the left of the dealer lays down any pairs in his hand and then asks any other player for a card he needs.

    Beginners might sign or fingerspell set phrases, i.e.:

    May I have _____ ?
    Do you have _____ ?
    I need _____ .
    I want _____ .

6. The other player must give up the card if he has it. If he does not have it he tells the player (in signs or fingerspelling) "Go to Hubby's Homonym's Hangout". (Pick a card from the center pile).

7. Play continues in like manner until all the cards are used up and all the pairs are made.

8. The person with the greatest number of pairs is the winner.

NOTE: Homonyms are words that <u>sound alike</u> to a hearing person although they may not be spelled alike. When these words also <u>look alike</u> on the lips to the hearing impaired, they are called Homophenes. The list of possible homophenes is many times longer than that of homonyms. This is because there are many more sounds that look alike on the lips than sound alike to the ears. The speech <u>sounds</u> that are homophenous (look alike) are:

f, v, ph
m, b, p, mb, mp
s, z, soft c
w, wh
sh, ch, j, soft g
d, t, n, nt, nd
k, hard c, hard g, ng

e.g. (blank - black; perch - birch; aid - ate; cap - gap; pat - mat - bat, etc.)

APPENDIX: HOMONYMS - HOMOPHENES

Column A	Column B	Column A	Column B
one	won	assent	ascent
son	sun	aught	ought
seem	seam	beach	beech
knot	not	here	hear
sale	sail	foul	fowl
buy	by	peal	peel
new	knew	rap	wrap
to	two - too	shone	shown
deer	dear	sleight	slight
eight	ate	stair	stare
blue	blew	some	sum
scent	cent - sent	throne	thrown
you	ewe	which	witch
wood	would	hall	haul
night	knight	all	awl
tail	tale	peak	peek
seen	scene	choose	chews
allowed	aloud	colonel	kernel
council	counsel	team	teem
draft	draught	die	dye
liar	lyre	guilt	gilt
profit	prophet	him	hymn
rough	ruff	raise (rays)	raze
sweet	suite	straight	strait
yoke	yolk	weight	wait
hair	hare	peer	pier
air	heir	braid	brayed
muscle	mussel	chute	shoot
earn	urn	guide	guyed
hues	hews	ewes	yews

APPENDIX: HOMONYMS - HOMOPHENES (Continued)

Column A	Column B	Column A	Column B
led	lead	coat	cote
missile (Missal)	mistle	none	nun
knead	need	done	dun
right	write	rain	reign
staid	stayed	road	rode
wig	whig	side	sighed
wine	whine	sight	site
bare	bear	wet	whet
pear (pair)	pare	wen	when
been	bin	medal (metal)	meddle
petal (pedal)	peddle	beat	beet
meat	meet	maze	maize
dew (do)	due	mote	moat
mown	moan	died	dyed
tide	tied	might	mite
feint	faint	vane	vein
made	maid	pain	pane
piece	peace	beat	beet
red	read	mane (Maine)	main
flour	flower	gait	gate
so	sew	break	brake
be	bee	ball	bawl
fare	fair	through	threw
whole	hole	four	for
bore	boar	row	roe

I.   OBJECTIVE: For the "human letters" to arrange themselves to correctly spell the given word.

II. VALUE: To increase visual perception and spacial relationships.

III. LEVEL: Beginning through advanced. (Children to adults)

IV. MODE: Fingerspelling or signs (receptive).

V.   MATERIALS NEEDED:

  1. Thinking caps.

VI. TO PLAY: (Best if 10 or more players)

  1. Assign each player a letter. Make sure to assign all the vowels. (A E I O U) as well consonants of high incidence. (B C D M N R S T Y). Players hold one hand (best if all players use the same hand) in the letter assigned.

  2. Teacher fingerspells or signs a word that contains some or all of the letters assigned.

  3. Players who have those letters quickly and silently arrange themselves to form the word. Remember it should read from the readers' left to right.

  4. Play continues in like manner with teacher rapidly giving words.

VARIATION I: Signed Sentences

  1. Choose one player to begin. That player starts by making one sign that could logically start sentence.

  2. Any player who so desires may then jump up and add another sign that makes sense.

  3. Third player now adds the third sign.

4. Play continues in like manner until a sentence is completed.

5. When sentence is complete all the players should be standing in a line. Then have the sentence repeated with each player repeating his sign. This repetition allows the reader to see the sentence as a whole instead of fragmented.

6. Play continues in like manner with players generating new sentences.

THE·IDIOM·ISSUE

I. <u>OBJECTIVE</u>: To correctly translate the English idioms into equivalent English phrases.

II. <u>VALUE</u>: To provide practice in rapid translation of English idioms into non-idiomatic phrases using Manually Coded English (MCE) or American Sign Language (ASL).

III. <u>LEVEL</u>: Intermediate and advanced. (Junior high school to adults)

IV. <u>MODE</u>: Fingerspelling and signs.

V. MATERIALS NEEDED:

1. Thinking caps.

2. Appendix.

3. For further materials:

a) A Dictionary of Idioms for the Deaf, compiled and edited by Maxine Tull Boatner, Ph.D. and John Edward Gates, B.D., S.T.M., American School for the Deaf, West Hartford, CN. 06107, 1966.

b) Conversational Sign Language II, An Intermediate-Advanced Manual. (Part II - English Idioms in Sign Language.) by Willard J. Madsen, Gallaudet College, Washington, D.C., 1972.

VI. <u>TO PLAY</u>:

1. Teacher chooses a group of idioms with meanings.

2. Teacher fingerspells an idiom and selects a player to sign or fingerspell a phrase that is equivalent.

3. Play continues in like manner.

<u>NOTE</u>: Very often it happens that an idiom is explained with another idiom. It is also true that it sometimes requires many more words to explain an idiom than are contained in the idiom itself.

APPENDIX: THE IDIOM ISSUE

1. ......ace in the hole... - something important kept as a surprise until the last minute.

2. ......add fuel to the fire... - make a bad situation worse.

3. ......after one's own heart... - to be liked because of agreeing with your own feelings.

4. ......along for the ride... - taking credit but doing none of the work.

5. ......apple of one's eye... - something that is loved or cherished.

6. ......ask for the moon... - try for something impossible.

7. ......at one's fingertips... - within easy reach.

8. ......beat around the bush... - to talk but never give an answer to the question.

9. ......bet on the wrong horse... - to misjudge a future event.

10. ......big frog in a small pond... - important person in a small group.

11. ......bite the hand that feeds one... - to turn against someone who helped you.

12. ......bolt from the blue... - something sudden.

13. ......champ at the bit... - eager to start doing something.

14. ......coast is clear... - no danger in sight.

15. ......do a double take... - to look twice in surprise.

16. ......fall over backwards... - to do anything to please someone.

17. ......get one's goat... - to make someone angry.

18. ......hard nut to crack... - something difficult to understand or do.

19. ......in the bag... - something sure to be won.

20. ......needle in the haystack... - something hard to find.

I. <u>OBJECTIVE</u>:   To guess the complete word when given the inword and a
clue.

II. <u>VALUE</u>:   To provide practice in thinking about groups of letters as being
part of a word.

III. <u>LEVEL</u>:   Beginning to advanced.   (Upper elementary to adults)
(Beyond beginning level, game is just for fun)

IV. <u>MODE</u>:   Fingerspelling and some signs.

V. <u>MATERIALS NEEDED</u>:

1. 1 game of INWORD published by Milton Bradley, Springfield, MA.,
1972.

VI. <u>TO PLAY</u>:

1. To play, follow directions that come on the box except that all
communication is signed and/or fingerspelled.

<u>VARIATION</u>:

1. To make a simplified version of this game, on 3x5 cards write
out words which contain <u>inwords</u>. The inword itself must be a
complete word. Devise a clue for the inword and write it under-
neath the <u>inword</u>.

2. One player acts as the leader who fingerspells the inword, and
the number of letters in the word.

e.g.   Bond

The inword is <u>on</u>.   The complete word has <u>4</u> letters.   The clue
is: "A substance which fuses."

3. Players in turn ask if a particular letter is in the words.   The
leader responds "yes" or "no".

4. When a player thinks he knows the word, he may guess when his
turn comes.

5. No scoring is necessary.

JUGGLING

I. <u>OBJECTIVE</u>: To create a new word by juggling the letters of a given word to fit a definition.

II. <u>VALUE</u>: To increase the ability to read fingerspelling and signs. The actual ability to create the <u>new</u> word is secondary to reading the given word and definition.

III. <u>LEVEL</u>: Intermediate to advanced students. (Junior high school to adults)

IV. <u>MODE</u>: Fingerspelling and signs.

V. <u>MATERIALS NEEDED</u>:

    1. Lists of words and definitions from Appendices A and B.

    2. Thinking caps.

VI. <u>TO PLAY</u>:

    1. Teacher or student teacher fingerspells one word from the list.

    2. Teacher explains that she/he will give a definition for a new word that can be spelled by juggling the letters of the first or given word.

    3. Teacher fingerspells and/or signs the definition. (Definition may contain several words).

    4. Students if they understood the given word and the definition will quickly find the new word.

APPENDIX: A) - JUGGLING

*Should be spelled not signed as signs are similar to the new word.

Given Word	Definition of the New Word	New Word
art	a rodent	rat
has	residue from a fire	ash
owe	*sad	woe
arm	male sheep	ram
ate	liquid to drink	tea
ink	relatives	kin
dad	*to increase	add
pot	spinning toy	top
pat	skilled	apt
two	to pull	tow
den	*finish	end
ape	vegetable	pea
erects	hidden knowledge	secret
groan	instrument	organ
robe	to drill	bore
leap	light in color	pale
ripe	dock	pier
tried	*weary	tired
smile	measured distance	miles
shore	large animal	horse
rate	a rip	tear
care	running *competition	race
left	a fabric	felt
are	time period	era
lead	*give out cards	deal
meat	players in a sport	team
nuts	to shock	stun
peal	*to jump	leap
spare	long knife	spear
name	*cruel	mean
praise	to hope for	aspire
mane	unkind	mean
cork	*a stone	rock
crate	to copy	trace
livers	shiny metal	silver

APPENDIX: B - JUGGLING (This group is all made from palindromes)

*Should be spelled not signed as signs are similar to the new word.

Given Word	Definition of the New Word	New Word
war	*not cooked	raw
won	*present time	now
stop	cooking utensils	pots
leer	a *spool for film	reel
ton	negative word	not
top	flower container	pot
deer	bamboo like grass	reed
room	to anchor	moor
keep	*to glance	peek
dam	*angry	mad
rat	sticky black substance	tar
dew	to marry	wed
evil	*to reside	live
tug	sheep entrails	gut
tops	a blot	spot
stool	*steals	loots
devil	*resided before	lived
bad	small amount	dab
dog	*a diety	god
bat	a projection	tab
tub	a conjunction	but
lap	*a friend	pal
pat	a light touch	tap
par	to knock	rap
leper	to oppose	repel
pins	*to cut	snip
loop	*billiards	pool
trap	*a portion	part
step	domestic animals	pets
star	rodents	rats
gas	to droop	sag
bus	prefix for under	sub
slap	friends	pals
spit	pointed ends	tips
brag	clothing	garb
was	cutting tool	saw
bag	to chatter	gab
mat	Scottish cap	tam
pay	bark	yap
no	upon	on
tool	spoils or booty	loot
nap	to wash gold	pan
'tis	occupy a seat	sit
tip	fruit stone	pit
tin	young insect	nit
ban	to seize	nab

APPENDIX: B) JUGGLING (Continued)

Given Word	Definition of the New Word	New Word
mid	indistinct	dim
pin	to pinch	nip
nod	to put on	don
mug	a chewing substance	gum
am	slang for mother	ma
net	a number	ten
mar	male sheep	ram
ward	to sketch	draw
tram	shopping place	mart
pans	break suddenly	snap
tang	small insect	gnat
flog	a game	golf
keel	a green vegetable	leek
emit	seconds, minutes, hours	time
laud	double purpose	dual
bard	dull	drab
warts	dried hay	straw
repaid	baby pants	diaper
drawer	prize	reward
retool	a robber	looter
tuber	argue	rebut
sleep	skin of fruits	peels
trams	intelligent	smart
timer	to send in	remit
revel	tool for lifting	lever

I.   OBJECTIVE: To collect as many matched pairs as possible.

II. VALUE: To provide a pleasurable way to practice already taught vocabulary.

III. LEVEL: Beginners and intermediate. (Elementary to adults)

IV. MODE: Fingerspelling and/or signs.

V.   MATERIALS NEEDED:

1. One set of NOUNTOWN, a Vocabulary Word Game by Karla Ross, Copyright 1973. 375 basic nouns divided into 25 decks arranged by category. Available from:

   Ross Educational Products
   P. O. Box 304
   Holes Corners, Wisconsin 53130

VI. TO PLAY:

Play game exactly as printed directions except that no speaking is allowed. All normally spoken dialogue is to be signed or fingerspelled.

VARIATION I:

1. Create your own decks of picture cards with matching word cards by using blank playing cards or by cutting 6x8 cards in half. This procedure will produce playing cards that are 4x3 just slightly larger than standard cards that are 3 1/2 x 2 1/2.

2. Use approximately 30 to 40 cards. On one half of the cards paste pictures of vocabulary that you desire to practice. On the other half of the cards,

    a. print the words that match the pictures or
    b. paste a picture of the sign if available, or
    c. paste the pictures of the manual alphabet for each word or
    d. paste different pictures of the same objects. (very good for young children).

3. Play the game according to the rules of FISH.

PREFIX PLUS

I. OBJECTIVE: To make a word that fits the definition using a given prefix.

II. VALUE: To increase ability to discriminate among fingerspelled words that start with identical letter groupings.

III. LEVEL: Beginning through advanced. (Junior high school through adults)

IV. MODE: Fingerspelling and/or signs.

V. MATERIALS NEEDED:

    1. Appendix.

    2. Thinking caps.

VI. TO PLAY:

    1. The teacher or student teacher fingerspells one of the prefixes from Appendix. Then a definition is fingerspelled or signed. The student is chosen or volunteers to answer by fingerspelling the new word.

APPENDIX: PREFIX PLUS

(Many more examples can be found in the dictionary)

PREFIX	DEFINITION	NEW WORD
	invent	compose
	collect	compile
COM	collate	compare
	instrument	compass
	exchange	commute
	stick	adhere
	coming	advent
AD	qualifier	adverb
	more forward	advanced
	to fit	adjust

APPENDIX: PREFIX PLUS (Continued)

PREFIX	DEFINITION	NEW WORD
	tell	inform
	bug	insect
IN	influence	inspire
	irrational	insane
	devise	invent
	trust	confide
	restrict	confine
CON	competition	contest
	evoke	conjure
	coagulate	congeal
	register	enroll
	adorn	enrich
EN	follow	ensue
	whole	entire
	bewitch	enchant
	dismiss	remove
	fix	repair
RE	quit	resign
	expose	reveal
	narrate	relate
	except	unless
	restless	uneasy
UN	sad	unhappy
	can't	unable
	release	unhook
	injure	impair
	levy	impose
IM	pierce	impale
	disclose	impart
	stamp	imprint
	(to) ready	prepare
	introduction	preface
PRE	apology	pretext
	fool	pretend
	give	present
	guide	conduct
	adapt	conform
CON	acknowledge	confirm
	perplex	confuse
	trust	confide

SCAVENGER HUNT

I. <u>OBJECTIVE</u>: To get the greatest number of items from the list.

II. <u>VALUE</u>: To read fingerspelling or signs with great rapidity and react immediately.

III. <u>LEVEL</u>: Beginning through advanced. (Upper elementary to adult)

IV. <u>MODE</u>: Fingerspelling or signs.

V. <u>MATERIALS NEEDED</u>:

1. Players who have their purses or wallets with them, <u>or</u>

2. Children in a classroom where a variety of items are around the room.

VI. <u>TO PLAY</u>:

1. Divide the group into 2 teams.

2. The teacher has a scavenger list prepared in advance. (See Appendix).

3. The teacher fingerspells or signs the first item on the list.

4. The first person on either team to run to the teacher with the item requested, makes a point for his/her team.

5. The team with the greater number of points wins the game.

APPENDIX: SCAVENGER HUNT

Suggested items for the list. All are commonly found in a purse, wallet or on the person.

pencil
pen
rainhat
nail clippers
scissors
pen knife
perfume
driver's license
social security card
trading stamp
Kennedy half dollar
a pocket knife
a picture of yourself

sugarless gum
Medical (insurance) cards
paper clip
picture of your grandchild
shoelace
safety pin
nail file
cancelled stamp
store receipt
credit card (specific varieties
                    gas, store)
a foreign coin

bobby pin
luggage key
1971 penny
a letter
a class ring
glasses
a bandaid
sunglasses
red pencil
a pill
a mirror
a bottle
      opener

NOTE: For children in a classroom situation, make the list according to availability of items.

I. <u>OBJECTIVE</u>: To collect as many matched pairs as possible and not be caught holding Sister Synonym.

II. <u>VALUE</u>: To provide practice in the signs for <u>English</u> synonyms or in fingerspelling.

III. <u>LEVEL</u>: Beginning or intermediate. (Children to adults)

IV. <u>MODE</u>: Signs or fingerspelling.

V. <u>MATERIALS NEEDED</u>:

1. Blank playing cards <u>or</u> 6x8 index cards cut in half. (As many as desired)

2. Words from the Appendix.

3. One Sister Synonym card.

4. Roget's Thesaurus for additional synonyms.

VI. <u>TO PLAY</u>:

1. Using word pairs or sets from the Appendix, write one word per card.

2. Xerox a copy of Sister Synonym. Cut out the copy and paste it on <u>one</u> card.

3. Prepare 20 to 30 cards for one deck plus one Sister Synonym card.

4. Shuffle and deal out five (5) cards per player. (2-4 players per game)

5. Put the remaining cards face down on the table. They are "Sister's House".

6. The player on the left of the dealer lays down any pairs in his hand and then asks any other player for a card he needs.

Beginners might sign or fingerspell set phrases, i.e.:

May I have _____ ?
Do you have _____?
I need _____ .
I want _____ .

7. The other player must give up the card if he has it. If he does not have it he tells the player (in signs or fingerspelling) "Go to Sister's House". (Pick a card from the center pile). Or if he has the Sister Synonym card in his hand he may quietly give that to the player instead as if it were the requested card.

8. Play continues in like manner until all the cards are used up and all the pairs (sets) are made.

9. The person with the greatest number of pairs is the winner and the person left with Sister Synonym becomes the one to deal the next hand or lead the next activity or whatever "prize" the teacher can devise for holding that "dubious distinction".

VARIATION I: (a reading only game for elementary school age children)

1. Play the game using the rules of Old Maid.

VARIATION II:

1. Use as a simple drill (without the cards) for reading sign or fingerspelling.

APPENDIX: SISTER SYNONYM

pretty - beautiful
address - residence
mansion - palace
cancel - abolish
abrupt - sudden
forgive - pardon
ridiculous - absurd (silly)
abundance - plenty (affluence)
control - manage (handle)
art - draw (design)
candidate - volunteer
important - worth (value)
fill - complete
advise - counsel
count - figure
taste - favorite (prefer)

talent - skill
ache - pain (hurt)
admit - confers (acknowledge)
agile - nimble (limber)
shake - tremble (quiver)
aid - help
glad - happy
wonderful - marvelous (fantastic)
make - fix (repair)
basement - cellar
cost - charge (fine)
spirit - soul (ghost)
ability - skill (expertness)
begin - start (initiate)
times - multiply

TWENTY QUESTIONS

I. OBJECTIVE: To guess the "item".

II. VALUE: To allow the questioners to use many of the signs they know, supplemented with fingerspelling in an unstructured setting.

III. LEVEL: Intermediate and advanced. (Junior high school to adults)

IV. MODE: Signs and fingerspelling.

V. MATERIALS NEEDED:

1. Thinking caps.

2. Items from Appendix.

VI. TO PLAY:

1. Choose one player to be the "owner" of the item.

2. The other players in turn ask questions (in signs or fingerspelling) of the owner. These questions must be designed to uncover the identity of the item and also the questions can only be answered with a "yes" or "no".

VARIATION I:

1. Divide players into teams.

2. Play as above except play alternates between the two teams.

3. Keep score of the number of questions asked - up to 20. After 20 questions the "owner" must tell what the item is if it has not already been guessed.

4. When a predetermined number of rounds are completed, add up the total number of questions asked by each team. Low score wins.

After this game is played several times, questioners will learn certain key questions that give a great amount of information and thereby save a lot of time.

e.g.	a. Is it animal?	No.
	b. Is it vegetable?	No.
	c. Is it mineral?	Yes.
	d. Is it used by men and women alike?	Yes.
	e. Is it still used today in 1977?	Yes.
	f. Is it found in the living room?	No.
	g. Is it found in the kitchen?	Yes.
	h. Is it bigger than a loaf of bread?	No.
	i. Is it used for cooking?	Yes.
	j. Is it hollow?	Yes.
	k. Does it have a handle?	Yes.
	l. Does it hold a variety of foods?	No.
	m. Does it hold anything consumable?	Yes.
	n. Does it hold solid food?	No.
	o. Does it hold liquid?	Yes.
	p. Is the liquid water?	Yes.
	q. Is it a teapot?	Yes.

APPENDIX: TWENTY QUESTIONS

<u>ITEMS</u>

roller skates
taxi cab
covered wagon
drawbridge
fan
electric knife
jigsaw puzzle
magnifying glass
clarinet
pipe wrench

a pet tarantula
a beehive
pocketbook
fishing rod
scrap book
horse shoe
cinnamon stick
storm window
tuning fork
elephant tusks

<u>ADD YOUR OWN</u>:

_____

_____

_____

_____

_____

_____

_____

_____

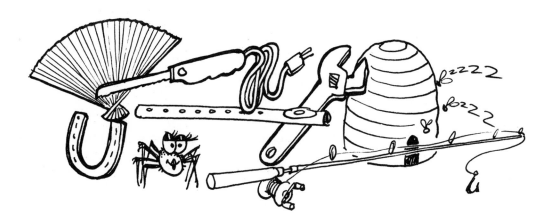

TELL IT LIKE IT IS !!
THE UNGAME

I. OBJECTIVE: To share thoughts, ideas and feelings and develop a deeper understanding of others and of self.

II. VALUE: To provide the opportunity for extemporaneous use and reading of signs and fingerspelling.

III. LEVEL: Intermediate through advanced. (Junior high school to adult)

IV. MODE: Fingerspelling and/or signs.

V. MATERIALS NEEDED:

1. One or more copies of the game called: TELL IT LIKE IT IS!! THE UNGAME (published and copyrighted in 1972 by

> AU-VID
> P.O. Box 964
> Garden Grove, CA 92642

Game has included within 2 decks of question cards:

a. yellow - for lighthearted fun.

b. white - to gain deeper understanding.

c. blank cards to add your own questions to these decks.

Optional specialized cards are available by additional order:

a. blue - questions submitted by students throughout the United States. For use by all ages.

b. green - questions for married couples submitted by marriage counselors and psychologists.

c. salmon - questions dealing with Christian belief submitted by Ministers.

VI. TO PLAY: (2-6 players per game)

1. Follow instructions included in the game box, except that all communication in the game is signed.

VOCABULARY REVIEW

I. OBJECTIVE: To use a given word correctly in a sentence.

II. VALUE: Provide instant use for newly learned vocabulary words.

III. LEVEL: Beginning through advanced. (Children to adults)

IV. MODE: Signs and "reversing".

V. MATERIALS NEEDED:

    1. Thinking caps.

    2. List of previously taught vocabulary. (Supplied by the teacher.)

VI. TO PLAY:

    1. Teacher fingerspells previously learned vocabulary words one at a time.

    2. As each one is given the teacher may choose a player to respond or he may volunteer. The player must then use the word in a sentence.

    3. Another player may be chosen or volunteer to reverse the signed sentence into spoken English.

NOTE: It is more difficult to do Step 3 from American Sign Language (ASL) into Spoken English than from Manually Coded English (MCE) into spoken English. Care must be taken not to reverse ASL into spoken ASL which then sounds like ungrammatical English.

67

I. OBJECTIVE: To guess the occupation of each player by asking questions.

II. VALUE: To provide subject oriented receptive material.

III. LEVEL: Intermediate to advanced. (Junior high school to adult)

IV. MODE: Signs and fingerspelling.

V. MATERIALS NEEDED:

    1. Thinking caps.

    2. Occupations from Appendix.

VI. TO PLAY:

    1. Choose an occupation from the list.

    2. Choose one player to have that occupation.

    3. Other players in turn ask questions that would require a "yes" or "no" answer in order to guess the person's occupation.

    4. If a player feels he knows the occupation he may at his turn make a guess instead of asking a question.

    5. Players continue asking questions in turn until the occupation is guessed.

    6. Choose another occupation and person and continue as above.

VARIATION I:

    1. Divide players into teams.

    2. Play as above except play alternates between the two (2) teams.

    3. Keep score of the number of questions asked for each occupation.

    4. When a predetermined number of rounds are completed, add up the total number of questions asked by each team. Low score wins.

(Occupation - Light Bulb Maker) e.g.

    a. Are you self-employed?   No.

    b. Do you work for a company?   Yes.

    c. Does this company produce more than one item?   No.

    d. Can this item be used by men and women?   Yes.

    e. Is it found indoors?   Yes.

    f. Is it found in only one room in the house?   No.

    g. Can it be found in every room of the house?   Yes.

    h. Is it a necessary item?   Yes.

    i. Is it small enough to hold in the hand?   Yes.

    j. Is it used more at one time of day than another?   Yes.

    k. Do you use it by itself?   No.

    l. Is it breakable?   Yes.

    m. Does its use produce a change in its environment?   Yes.

    n. Do you touch it when you use it?   No.

    o. Does it give off heat?   Yes.

    p. Is it a light bulb?   Yes.

    q. Are you an electrician?   No.

    r. Do you make light bulbs?   Yes.

APPENDIX: WHAT'S MY LINE

Occupations:

Write Your Own

barber
florist
sign painter
blacksmith
bricklayer
architect
lawyer
doctor
secretary
seamstress
actress/actor
zoo curator
violin maker
pro-hockey player
plumber

department store Santa
animal trainer
chef
computer programmer
author
dental technician
shoemaker
stewardess
photographer
artist
newscaster
printer
choreographer
conductor (orchestra)
minister

_____
_____
_____
_____
_____
_____
_____
_____
_____
_____
_____
_____
_____
_____

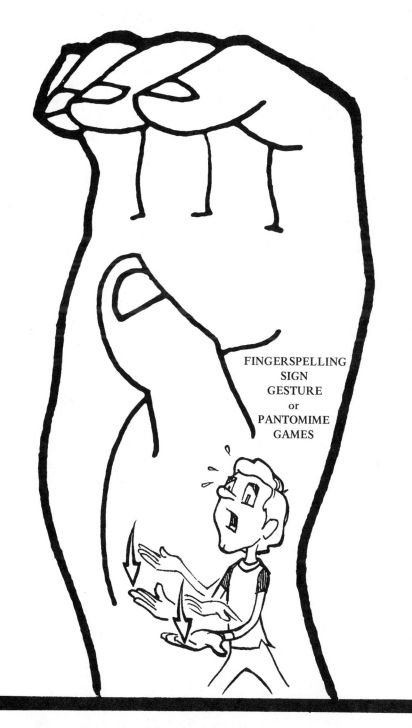

FINGERSPELLING
SIGN
GESTURE
or
PANTOMIME
GAMES

ASSOCIATIONS

I. __OBJECTIVE__: To give as many words in fingerspelling or sign that are associated with a given topic.

II. __VALUE__: To stretch the ability to "read" vocabulary associated with a topic of conversation. Use as a recall exercise or to determine the number of signs known in a category.

III. __LEVEL__: Intermediate to advanced. (Junior high school to adults)

IV. __MODE__: Sign and/or fingerspelling and pantomime.

V. MATERIALS NEEDED:

    1. Lists of topics (see Appendix).

    2. Thinking caps.

VI. __TO PLAY__:

METHOD A. Team Play

    1. Divide group into two (2) teams and arrange them so they cannot see each other.

    2. Choose a topic and assign it to each team. Both teams work on the same topic.

    3. Each team chooses a captain who writes the associations on the board or a larger sheet of paper.

    4. A time limit is set.

    5. Members of the group take turns signing or spelling words associated with the topic which the captain records.

    6. The team with the highest number of legitimate associations is the winner.

METHOD B. One Group Play

    1. Play as in METHOD A except there is only one captain to record the associations offered by the members of the group.

    2. There is no scoring.

APPENDIX:

(Choose an individual item from any of these categories).

1. A sport   (baseball, tennis, football, horseracing, track, basketball, etc.)

2. An animal   (cat, dog, fish, lion, horse, elephant, whale, etc.)

3. A season   (winter, spring, summer, fall)

4. Occupations   (secretary, teacher, lawyer, doctor, engineer, nurse, fireman, policeman)

5. Places   (countries, states, museums, amusement parks, national parks)

6. Holidays   (New Years, Valentine's Day, Easter, Passover, July 4th, Halloween, Thanksgiving, Chanukkah, Christmas)

e.g. TOPIC: <u>HORSERACING</u>

   ASSOCIATIONS: Horse, rider, saddle, boots, silks, crop (whip), spurs, blinders, reins, stirrups, track, weight, flat, sulky, bet, money, roses, silver cup, fast, muddy, etc.

INTRODUCTION·GAME

I. <u>OBJECTIVE</u>: To introduce new members in the class and learn something about each one.

II. <u>VALUE</u>: To increase visual memory.

III. <u>LEVEL</u>: Beginning through advanced. (Children to adults)

IV. <u>MODE</u>: Pantomime, signs or fingerspelling.

V. <u>MATERIALS NEEDED</u>:

    1. Thinking caps.

    2. Appendix for "fact" ideas.

VI. <u>TO PLAY</u>:

    1. The first player introduces himself (note <u>Mode</u> above) by stating his name and another fact about himself.

    2. The next player repeats what the first player has done and adds his own name and fact.

    3. The third player repeats the information from the second and adds his own.

    4. Introductions continue in like manner with each person repeating the information of the person just before them, plus his own, until all are completed.

<u>VARIATION I</u>:

    1. Have each person repeat all those who went before him. (Use this only if the group is small).

<u>VARIATION II</u>:

    1. Use the format of your choice but allow <u>no</u> signing or finger-spelling or writing. Instead use all pantomime. The name (first, last or both) must be communicated in some non-verbal way as well as the fact. The name can be printed in air, formed with the body, acted out if it has a double meaning, etc. The facts are more easily done by pantomime, pointing, gesturing, etc.

APPENDIX: INTRODUCTION GAME

1. My name is _____ and I like _____ .

2. My name is _____ and I come from _____ .

3. My name is _____ and my hobby is _____ .

4. My name is _____ and my favorite color is _____ .

5. My name is _____ and my favorite food is _____ .

6. My name is _____ and I'd like to visit _____ .

7. My name is _____ and I'd like to be (a) _____ .

8. My name is _____ and I think _____ is fun.

9. My name is _____ and my job is _____ .

10. My name is _____ and my favorite charity is _____ .

I. OBJECTIVE: To accurately pass a message (tactile, gestured, finger-spelled or signed) from the first person to the last person in line.

II. VALUE: To increase awareness at all levels and the ability to accurately reproduce that which is seen or felt.

III. LEVEL: Beginning and intermediate. (Children to adults)

IV. MODE: Tactile impressions, gestures, fingerspelling or signs.

V. MATERIALS NEEDED:

    1. A method from the Appendix.

    2. Thinking caps.

VI. TO PLAY:

    1. Arrange players in a straight line, either seated or standing. Players not involved in the message should not be able to see the two persons who are.

    2. The message may be originated by the first person in line or the teacher.

    3. The first person passes the "message" to the second person. The message is given only one time. The receiver must understand the message as best he/she can and pass it on in exactly the same way.

4. The second person passes the message to the third person - the third to the fourth etc. - until the last person receives the message.

5. The last person may repeat the message for all to see and each may compare that to what he/she received and sent. (Laughter often occurs here especially with beginners).

APPENDIX: TELEPHONE GAMES

Methods for creating messages.

1. Tactile (done while receiver is watching or has eyes closed).

    a. draw a letter or word in the palm of the hand.

    b. tap a morse code pattern in the palm of the hand.
    (e.g. _ _.._.)

    c. touch various parts of the hand in a pattern.
    e.g. touch tip of thumb, center of palm, end of index finger,
    end of ring finger, the center of palm again).

    d. fingerspell a short word slowly into the palm of receiver allow-
    ing him/her to feel the configuration of the letters (as a deaf/
    blind person would do).

2. Gestures

    a. give a pattern of gestures.

        1) using hands only.

        2) hands touching head, shoulders, etc.

3. Fingerspelling

    a. a short word

    b. a short phrase

    c. a short sentence

4. Signs

    a. single signs - particularly those which are similar in hand-
    shape (dez) and/or location (tab) or movement (sig) that might
    easily be misunderstood and therefore repeated wrongly.

        e.g. 1) apple, onion, aunt, female, etc.

             2) meet, to, goal, etc.

             3) salt, train, sit, etc.

    b. a short phrase in signs

        1) composed of signs similar in handshape (dez) and/or loca-
        tion (tab) or movement (sig).

        2) composed of signs that don't make sense together.

c. sentences in signs

1) nonsense sentences which are difficult to remember.

2) sentences containing factual information, especially dates.

3) sentences containing quotes (eg. My mother said, " ___ __

___ __ ___ ".)

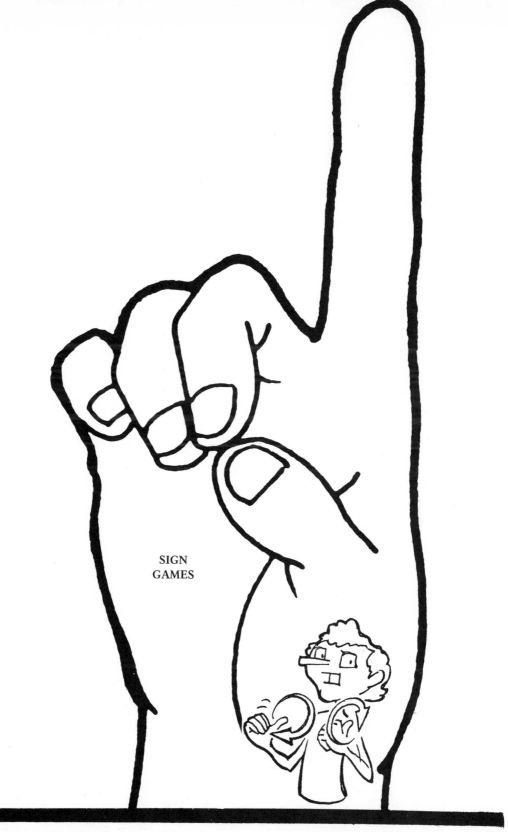

SIGN
GAMES

The Dez Game

I. OBJECTIVE: To do as many signs using the same dez (hand shape) as possible.

II. VALUE: To create awareness of the similarity of many signs.

III. LEVEL: Beginning through advanced. (Upper elementary to adult)

IV. MODE: Signs

V. MATERIALS NEEDED:

  1. Thinking caps.

  2. Reference lists in Appendices.

VI. TO PLAY:

  1. Teacher chooses one handshape for play.

  2. Players take turns in order or at random, giving individual signs that are made with the selected handshape.

  3. This activity provides an opportunity for structural analysis of the parameters of signs. These parameters are:

   a. TAB - the place where the sign is made (face, trunk, chin, etc.)

   b. DEZ - the configuration of the hand or hands making the sign. ("A" hand - flat, "O" - "3" hand, etc.)

   c. SIG - the motion the sign makes. (upward, circular, linking, side to side, etc.)

NOTE: In the Appendix these basic signs have been arranged by their primary dez
        (hand configuration). These lists cover dez's from A to Y. Some signs
        could be listed under more than one, such as Hospital (H, N, U). These
        were placed abitrarily on just one list. Signs that move from one dez
        to another have been eliminated, such as hotdog (c to s - c to s). Very
        few signs from Manually Coded English systems and no technical signs have been
        included. There are no lists for dez's other than the alphabet. More
        complete lists would include lists for:

            the index hand
            the three or cock hand
            the horns hand
            the flat "0" or tapered hand, etc.

For further basic information consult:

            Dictionary of American Sign Language, by William C. Stokoe, Jr.,
            Dorothy C. Casterline, Carl G. Croneberg, 1965, Gallaudet College
            Press, Gallaudet College Bookstore, 7th and Florida Aves., N.E.
            Washington, DC 20002.

It is hoped that those who teach MCE would expand these lists to include
the large number of initialized signs in those systems. Also, because many
signs have regional variations in dez, some readers may wonder why some
signs are listed under a certain dez. The classifications by dez are
purely that of the author.

APPENDIX: THE "DEZ" GAME

<u>"A" HAND</u>

address
able
act (drama)
Adam
Africa
algebra
ambition
annoint
another
any
apple
area
army
associate
attempt
attitude
aunt
authority
bath
behind
blame
boast
brush
can
Canada
cards
change
chore
chew
coat
cracker
daily
direct
each
else
every

establish
farther
follow
girl
hide
___self (ves)
India
most
not (don't)
pass
patience
practice
proud
race
refuse
reign
secret
soldier
sorry
suffer
substitute
together
tomorrow
under
wash
which
with (out)
yesterdays
ten
celebrate
challenge
game
gas
sculpture
surgery
science

APPENDIX:

across	floor
after	forgive
afternoon	full
against	God
alright	good
allow	hands
arrange	have finish
autumn	hello
baby	here
bachelor	house
bad	humble
basic	improve
be	individual
beer	into
below	know
before	let
blue	line (of work)
boat	maybe
born	morning
bother	never
box	noon
bread	open
bring	paint
broke (money)	part
brown	pie
brought	plan
build	proof
bury	quiet
business	satisfied
busy	some
buy	stop
carry	sweet
center	superintendent
cheap	table
city	than
close	town
corner	trouble
concentrate	warn
dead	way
divide	worry
donkey	
door	
enter	
even	
excuse	
fall (season)	

"C" HAND

action
brilliant
boss (captain)
cabbage
cake
calendar
call
chapter
character
Chicago
chocolate
Christ
Christmas
church
class
commandment
communicate
complain
concept
cop
cousin
cream
cross
culture
cup
do
drink
examination (Physical)
hear
hot
hungry
hunt
listen
look (for)
marry
moon
much
odd
paragraph
picture
strange

"D" HAND

democrat
Denmark
design
develop
diamond
dictionary
divorce
doctor
duty

"E" HAND

east
engagement
evaluation

"F" HAND

choose
decide
describe
explain
family
foreign
France
free
fruit
function
if
important
Indian
judge
language
minister
Mass
pick
postpone
preach
precise
profit
replace
sentence
soul
spirit

"G" HAND

bird
Gallaudet
geometry
gospel
gossip
grace
graduate
grammar
Greek
green
group

"H" HAND	"J" HAND	"M" HAND	"P" HAND
butter	Japan	doctor	parents
Catholic	jealous	mathematics	party
fun	jelly	middle	pay
funny		missionary	people
history		Monday	perceive
holy			perfect
honest			permit
honor			person
hospital			personality
increase			philosophy
name			pink
nurse			place
paint			poem
salt	"K" HAND	"N" HAND	population
secretary			principal
short	borrow	nation	principle
signature	king	neice	program
	lend	nephew	psychiatrist
		normal	pure
		Norway	purple
		nurse	

"I" HAND	"L" HAND	"O" HAND	"Q" HAND
art			
I (pronoun)			
idea	big	objective	queen
idiom	language	teach	priest
imagine	large		turkey
individual	law		
institution	lawyer		
insurance	lazy		
interest	let		
island	library		
Israel	life		
Italy	Lord		

"R" HAND

rabbi
ready
reason
receptive
register
repetition
represent,
require
respect
response
responsible
rest
role
rule

"T" HAND

team
temple
theory
time (abstract)
toilet
traditional
try

"U" HAND

paint
register
 (sign a book)
salt
sweet
uncle
university
us
use

"S" HAND

advertise
attempt
beak
break
baseball
coffee
cold
defend
doubt
exaggerate
fight
free (verb)
habit
ice cream
lock
make
save
senate
shoes
situation
society

support
Sweden
symbol
thunder
winter
work
explode
year

"V" HAND

arithmetic
borrow
careful
careless
fail
fork
funeral
keep
ignorant
loan
look
means
misunderstand

multiply
prophet
purpose
read
save (keep)
see
stand
supervise
verb
vocabulary
voice
watch
worse

APPENDIX: THE "DEZ" GAME (Continued)

"W" HAND

Washington
water
we
wine
world

"X" HAND

dry
dull
Egypt
electricity
expression
friend
from
gift
hockey
lock (verb)
must
necessary
need
onion
puzzled
require
ruin (spoil)
should
summer
suspect
tease
tempt
time
ugly
wise

"Y" HAND

airplane
continue
country
foolish
last (remain)
measure
mistake
orange
play (verb)
razor
same
shave
silly
similar
stay
still
telephone
that
yellow
yes (yeah)
yesterday
yet
why
wrong

Poetic License

I. <u>OBJECTIVE</u>: To properly translate the Haiku poetry from its English translation into American Sign Language (ASL; Ameslan).

II. <u>VALUE</u>: To provide practice pieces that are short and very descriptive. This is especially important for beginners.

III. <u>LEVEL</u>: Beginning through advanced. (ASL Classes <u>only</u>)

IV. <u>MODE</u>: American Sign Language (these poems <u>could</u> be done in Manually Coded English but they would "lose <u>much</u> in this form of translation.")

V. <u>MATERIALS NEEDED</u>:

  1. Poems from the Appendix.

VI. <u>TO PLAY</u>:

  1. Choose poems from the Appendix and work out the ASL translations on an individual or group basis.

<u>NOTE</u>: This activity is only recommended for teachers who have <u>thorough</u> knowledge of American Sign Language (ASL). It is not <u>particularly</u> suited for classes in any form of Manually Coded English (MCE). Teachers who have normal hearing might benefit from reviewing their translations into ASL with a teacher or other individuals who are deaf.

APPENDIX: POETIC LICENSE - HAIKU

A haiku is a type of poetry from Japan. In Japanese, it has only seventeen (17) syllables. The Japanese call haiku "one-breath" poems because they are so short and have no rhyme. Each poem describes <u>one</u> feeling or <u>one</u> moment.

A drop of rain!
    the frog wiped his forehead
  with his wrist.

                    (Issa)

Grasshopper,
    Do not trample to pieces
  the pearls of bright dew.

                    (Issa)

APPENDIX: POETIC LICENSE - HAIKU

The moon in the water
        turned a somersault
and floated away.
                (Ryota)

Stillness:
        The sound of the petals
sifting down together.
                (Chora)

The frog
        is having a starring match
with me.
                (Issa)

A giant firefly:
        that way, this way, that way, this -
and it passes by.
                (Issa)

Ha! the butterfly!
        - it is following the person
who stole the flowers!
                (Anonymous)

With the evening breeze
        the water laps against
the heron's legs.
                (Buson)

On a rainy day
        the innkeeper
assigns even a horse
        a room.
                (Issa)

You can make a foggy, rainy day,
        into a sunny, bright, day
        when there is a friend to share
        it with.
                (Andrea)

On a rainy day
        it feels so good
        to see rain again.
                (C.J.)

A single mat
        beneath
a pine tree
        makes a summer mansion.
                (Issa)

On a rainy day
        all the plants
        grow taller.
                (Stacy)

The first firefly.....
        But he got away
        and I
        Air in my fingers.

I scooped up the moon
        in my water
        bucket...and
Spilled it on the grass.

The sickly orchid
        that I tended so....
        At last
Thanks me with a bud

With the moon rising....
        leaf after leaf
        after leaf
Falls fluttering down.

On the last long road
        when I fall and
        fail to rise...
I'll bed with flowers.

APPENDIX: POETIC LICENSE - HAIKU

My eyes following
   until the bird
    was lost at sea
found a small island.

Ah the falling snow...
   imagine dancing
    butterflies flitting
through the flakes!

Under a Spring mist,
   ice and water
    forgetting
their old difference...

The sun has gone down
   beyond a dead tree
    clutching
an old eagle's nest.

High on a mountain
   we heard a skylark
    singing faintly
far below...

The steaming river
   has washed the hot
    round red sun
down under the sea.

Too curious flower
   watching us pass,
    met death...
Our hungry donkey.

Fireworks ended
   and spectators
    gone away...
Oh, How vast and dark!

All night the ragged
   clouds and wind
    had only one
companion...The moon.

We rowed into fog,
   and out through fog...
    O how blue
How bright the wide sea!

A crow clings silent
   to a bare bough,
    cautiously
watching the sunset.

One fallen flower
   returning to the
    branch?...Oh No!
White butterfly.

Arise from sleep, old cat,
   and with great yawns
    and stretching
amble out for love.

Lightning flash, crash...
   waiting in the
    bamboo grove
see three dew-drops fall.

A saddening world:
   Flowers whose sweet
    blooms must fall...
As we too, Alas....

Rain.
Little pieces of glass
   falling from nowhere
in the sky.
       (9 year old deaf child)

APPENDIX:

SEASONS
  by Dorothy Miles

Spring

Sunshine, borne on breeze
among singing trees, to dance
rippled water.

Summer

Green depths and green heights
clouds and quiet hours - slow, hot,
heavy on the hands.

Autumn

Scattered leaves, a-whirl
in playful winds, turn to watch
people hurry by.

Winter

Contrast: black and white;
bare trees, covered ground; hard ice,
soft snow; birth in death.

(Used by permission - Gestures - Dorothy Miles - Joyce Media Inc. 1976)

SHAPE STORIES

I. OBJECTIVE: To create a story when presented with a shape stimulus.

II. VALUE: To trigger the imagination and to learn to visualize the <u>basic</u> shape of an object, or cluster of objects.

III. LEVEL: Beginning through advanced. (Children to adults)

IV. MODE: Speech and/or signs used to tell the story created by the player.

V. MATERIALS NEEDED:

1. Cardboard shapes in a <u>variety</u> of sizes and colors.

e.g.

etc.

VI. TO PLAY:

1. The first player chooses a shape and tells what it looks like to him.

2. The second player chooses a second shape - places it next to the first and then adds to the explanation or story.

3. Play continues in like manner until:

<u></u>   a. teacher determines it shall end,
<u>or</u> b. story has come to an obvious conclusion,
<u>or</u> c. shapes are exhausted.

e.g.

1. This is a triangle.
2. And now it's a house.
3. With a cloud soon to dump rain on that house.

A cat created from two circles, 2 triangles and 1 rectangle.

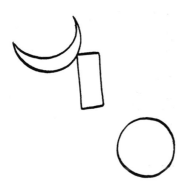

1. Here's a sliver of a moon.
2. With a Milky Way candy bar hanging off the corner.
3. And here's all the people on earth trying to get all those Milky Ways.

VARIATIONS

1. Have one person make the entire story or picture, adding shapes as he/she goes along.

2. Have several small groups each create a story or picture using a similar series of shapes.

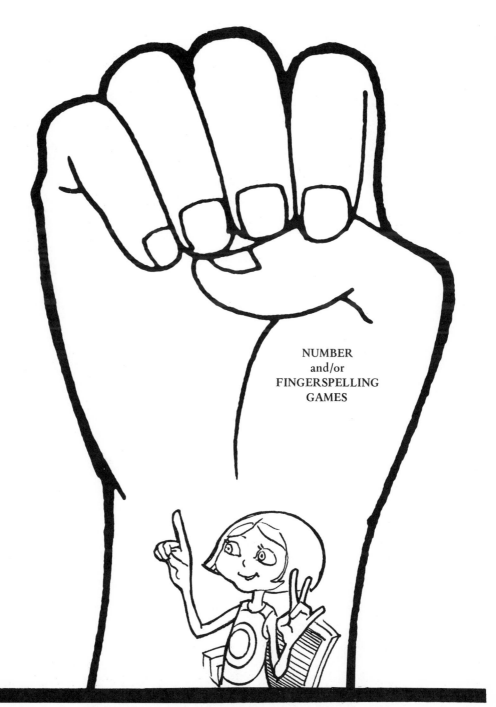

NUMBER
and/or
FINGERSPELLING
GAMES

I. <u>OBJECTIVE</u>: To make the highest number of words and therefore the highest score.

II. <u>VALUE</u>: To provide practice in doing and reading single letters of the alphabet and the Numbers 1 through 25.

III. <u>LEVEL</u>: Beginning through advanced. (Upper elementary to adult)

IV. <u>MODE</u>: Fingerspelling and numbers.

V. <u>MATERIALS NEEDED</u>:

1. Thinking caps.

2. Enough copies of the "COPY ME" sheets to supply class. - one per player.

3. Pencils.

VI. <u>TO PLAY</u>: (4 players per game)

1. Each player randomly writes the Numbers 1 through 25 on the blocks on Square A. Numbers should be small and in the upper left corner of each block.

2. Then the player numbers the blocks in Square B. - also at random but different from Square A.

3. Select one player to begin the game.

4. That player fingerspells a letter and a number.

5. <u>Each</u> player writes that letter in the block bearing the called number (on either Square A and B).

6. The next player fingerspells a letter and a number and again all players write it in the called block in either square.

7. Play continues in like manner with each player calling letters to his advantage to make words for himself and maybe to the disadvantage of others.

8. The game is finished when all the blocks on both squares are filled. Words are then counted and the winner is the one with the highest score.

The Rules of DOUBLE CROSSWORD:

1. All words must begin at the top for "down" words and at the far left for "across" words.

2. A player may call a "blank" and a number. When this occurs each player blackens the called block on either square. Blanks may separate 2 small words on the same line. Two small words not separated by blanks cannot count in the final score. (See illustration).

3. Words must be in the dictionary. They may not be proper names, abbreviations, foreign words or hyphenated words.

4. The words "I" and "A" are legal even though only one letter each.

To Score:

1. Count one point per letter of each made word. - first down each row and then across each row.

2. Then add up the totals from all the DOWN rows and then from all the ACROSS rows on Square A.

3. Repeat Step 2 for Square B.

4. Add up the 4 totals to gain the grand total.

5. The player with the highest grand total is the winner.

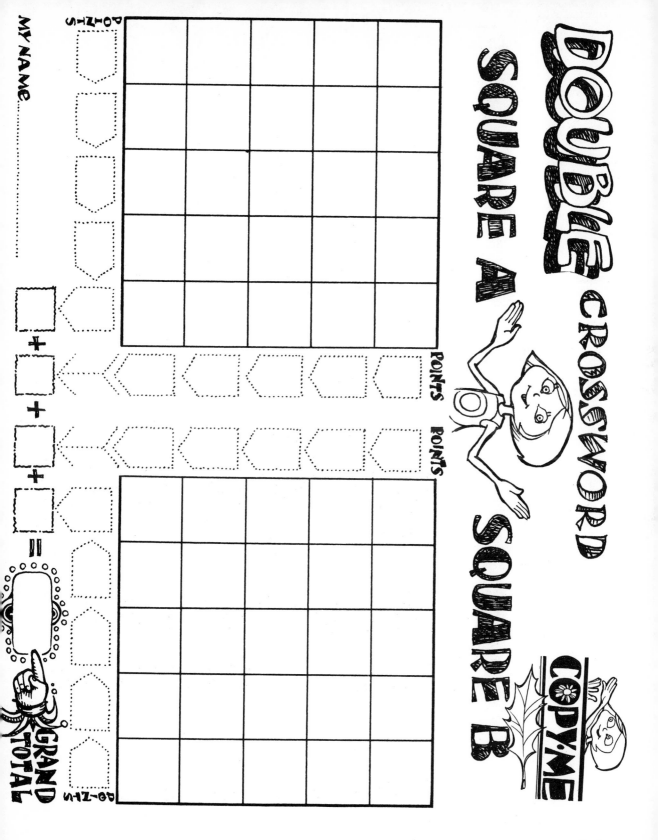

DOUBLE CROSSWORD

SQUARE A

SQUARE B

MY NAME ....

POINTS

POINTS

POINTS

□ + □ + □ + □ =

GRAND TOTAL

COPY ME

I. OBJECTIVE: To fill in the crossword puzzle.

II. VALUE: To provide receptive practice for fingerspelled or signed 3, 4 or 5 letter words as well as basic numbers. Could be an evaluation tool.

III. LEVEL: Beginning and Intermediate.

IV. MODE: Fingerspelling (sometimes signs).

V. MATERIALS NEEDED:

1. Sufficient copies of the "Copy Me" page for each player.

2. Words chosen from lists in Appendices. A - 3 letter words, B - 4 letter words, and C - 5 letter words.

VI. TO PLAY:

1. Distribute "Copy Me" pages to players.

2. Teacher chooses words from list - enough to complete the puzzle.

3. The teacher fingerspells a number and the word d-o-w-n or a-c-r-o-s-s. Allow student to locate the place on the "Copy Me" page.

4. Then fingerspell (or sign) the word that fits in those spaces.

5. Continue in like manner until the puzzle is completed.

NOTE: 1. For ease in playing, the teacher should completely work out a puzzle in advance.

2. Take note of corner words where the beginning letter is common to the word across and the word down.

3. The words in the Appendices are alphabetically arranged. For more words of any initial letter just continue with the last word using any standard dictionary.

APPENDIX: A DOWN AND ACROSS — 3 Letter Words

A	B	C	D	E	F	G	H
ace	bad	cab	dab	ear	fad	gag	had
act	bag	can	dad	eat	fag	gal	hag
aft	ban	cap	den	ebb	fan	gap	ham
age	bar	car	dew	eel	far	gay	has
ail	bat	cat	did	egg	fat	gem	hat
aim	bay	cob	die	eke	fed	get	hay
air	bed	cod	dig	elf	fee	gin	hem
ale	bee	cog	dim	elk	fen	god	hen
all	beg	cot	dip	err	few	got	her
and	bet	cow	dog	eve	fib	gum	hew
ant	bib	coy	don	eye	fig	gun	hey
any	bid	cry	dot		fin	gut	him
ape	big	cub	dry		fir	guy	hip
apt	bin	cud	dub		fit	gym	his
arc	bit	cue	dug		fix		hit
are	bob	cup	dye		fly		hoe
ark	bog	cut			foe		hog
arm	boo				fog		hop
art	bow				for		hot
ask	box				fry		

I	J	K	L	M	N	O	P
ice	jam	keg	lad	mad	nag	oaf	pad
icy	jar	ken	lag	man	nap	oak	pal
ill	jaw	key	lap	map	nay	oat	pan
imp	jay	kid	law	mar	net	odd	par
ivy	jet	kin	lax	mat	new	ode	paw
	jib		lay	maw	nip	off	pea
	jig		led	may	nod	oil	peg
	job		lee	mid	nor	old	pen
	jog		leg	mix	not	one	pep
	jot		let	mob	now	orb	per
	joy		lid	moo	nun	ore	pet
	jug		lie	mop	nut	our	pew
	jut		lip	mow		out	pie
			lit	mud		owe	pig
			log	mug		owl	pin
			low	mum		own	pit
							ply
							pod
							pop
							pry

APPENDIX: A DOWN AND ACROSS - 3 Letter Words (Continued)

R	S	T	U	V	W	Y	Z
rag	sac	tag	ugh	vex	wad	yak	zip
ram	sad	tan	use	via	wag	yam	zoo
ran	sag	tap			wan	yap	
rap	sap	tar			war	yen	
rat	sat	tax			was	yes	
raw	saw	the			wax	yet	
ray	say	tin			way	yew	
red	sea	tip			web	yon	
rib	set	toe			wed		
rid	sew	ton			wet		
rig	sex	too			who		
eim	she	top			wig		
rod	sip	tow			win		
roe	sir	toy			wit		
row	sit	try			wry		
rub	six	tug					
rum	sky	two					
run	sly						
rut	sow						
rye	spy						

A	B	C	D	E	F	G	H
able	babe	cafe	daft	each	face	gage	hack
ably	baby	cage	dale	earl	fact	gain	hail
ache	back	cake	dame	earn	fade	gait	hair
acid	bail	calf	damp	ease	fail	gale	hale
acne	bait	call	dank	east	fair	gall	half
afar	bake	calm	dare	echo	fake	game	hall
aged	bald	came	dark	eddy	fall	gang	halo
ahoy	bale	camp	darn	edge	fame	gape	halt
airy	balk	cane	dart	edit	fare	garb	hand
ajar	ball	cape	dash	emit	farm	gash	hang
alas	balm	card	data	envy	fast	gasp	hank
ally	band	care	date	epic	fate	gate	hard
alms	bang	carp	daub	etch	faun	gave	hare
also	bank	cart	dawn	even	fawn	gaze	hark
alto	barb	case	daze	ever	feat	gear	harp
alum	bard	cash	dead	evil	feed	germ	hart
amen	bare	cell	deaf	exit	feel	gibe	hash
amid	bark	cent	deal		feet	gift	hasp
anew	barn	chap	dear		fell	gild	hate
anon	base	chat	debt		felt	gilt	haul

I	J	K	L	M	N	O	P
idea	jake	kale	lace	mace	nail	oath	pace
idle	jade	keel	lack	made	name	obey	pack
idly	jail	keen	lacy	Magi	nape	obit	page
idol	jazz	keep	lady	maid	nave	odds	paid
inch	jean	kelp	laid	mail	near	ogre	pail
inky	jeep	kept	lain	maim	neat	oily	pain
into	jerk	kick	lair	main	neck	oleo	pair
iris	jest	kill	lake	make	need	omen	pale
iron	join	kiln	lamb	male	neon	once	pall
itch	joke	kilo	lame	mall	nest	only	palm
item	jolt	kilt	lamp	malt	news	onto	pane
	jowl	kind	land	mane	newt	onyz	pang
	jump	kink	lane	many	next	ooze	pant
	junk	kiss	lank	mare	nice	opal	park
	jury	kite	lark	mark	nick	open	parr
	just	knee	lash	mart	nill	opus	part
	jute	know	lass	mash	nine	orgy	pass
			last	mask	Noah	oryx	past
			late	mass	node	otic	pave

Q	R	S	T	U	V	W	Y
quad	race	sack	tabu	ugly	vain	wade	yank
quit	rack	safe	tack	unto	vale	waff	yard
quiz	raft	sage	tact	upon	vave	waft	yarn
	rage	said	tail	urge	vary	wage	yawl
	raid	sail	take		vase	waif	year
	rail	sake	talc		vast	wait	yelp
	rain	sale	tale		veal	wake	yoga
	rake	salt	talk		veer	wale	yoke
	ramp	same	tall		veil	walk	yolk
	rang	sand	tame		vein	wall	yore
	rank	sash	tamp		vend	wand	your
	rant	save	tang		vent	wane	yowl
	rare	scab	tank		verb	want	yule
	rash	scan	tape		very	ward	
	rasp	scar	tart		vest	ware	
	rate	seal	task		veto	warm	
	rave	seam	taut		vial	warn	Z
	raze	sear	team		vice	warp	
	read	seat	tear		view	wart	zany
	real	sect	teem		vile	wash	zeal
							zero
							zest
							zinv
							zing
							zone
							zoom

A	B	C	D	E	F	G	H
aback	bacon	cabby	daddy	eager	fable	gabby	habit
abase	baggy	cabin	daffy	eagle	facet	gable	hairy
abash	banjo	cable	daily	early	faint	gaily	halve
abate	barge	cacao	dairy	earth	famed	galop	handy
abbey	baron	cache	daisy	easel	fancy	gamut	haroy
abbot	basal	caddy	dally	eaves	farce	gaudy	haste
abhor	bases	cadet	dance	edict	fatal	gauge	hasty
abide	basic	cagey	daunt	edify	fault	gaunt	hatch
abode	basil	camel	dealt	educe	fauna	gavel	haunt
abort	basin	cameo	death	egret	favor	gawky	haven
about	basis	candy	debar	eight	feast	genus	hazel
above	baste	caper	debit	eject	feign	ghost	heart
abuse	batch	carat	debut	elate	feint	ghoul	heath
abyss	bathe	carob	decal	elbow	felon	giant	heavy
acorn	batik	caret	decor	elder	fence	giddy	hedge
acrid	baton	cargo	decoy	elegy	ferry	gland	hefty
actor	beard	carol	decry	elide	fetch	glare	hence
acute	beach	carry	defer	elite	fetid	glass	heron
adage	beech	caste	deity	elope	fever	glaze	hinge
adapt	befit		delay	elves	fiber	glean	
adept				emery			

I	J	K	L	M	N	O	P
idler	jabot	kapok	lable	madly	naked	obese	padre
igloo	jaded	kappa	labor	magic	nasal	occur	pagan
image	jaunt	karat	ladle	major	nasty	ocean	paint
impel	jelly	kayak	laird	mamma	natal	often	pansy
incur	jerky	keyed	lance	mange	navel	olive	paper
incus	jetty	kinky	lanky	mango	needs	opera	parch
index	jewel	kitty	large	mangy	needy	orbit	parka
inept	jiffy	knead	larva	manic	neigh	order	parry
inert	jimmy	kneel	latch	manly	nerve	organ	party
infer	joint	knell	lathe	manor	nervy	other	paste
inlay	joist	knock	laugh	manse	niche	otter	patch
inlet	joker	knurl	layer	maple	nifty	ought	paten
input	jolly	koala	leafy	march	night	ounce	pause
irate	joust	kodak	learn	marry	nihil	outdo	peach
islet	judge	krona	lease	mason	ninth	overt	pearl
issue	jumpy	krone	leash	maybe	nippy	ovule	pedal
itchy			least	meaty	noble	owner	peeve
			leave	medal	nomad	ozone	pekoe
			ledge	media	noose		pence
			leech	medic			

APPENDIX: C

DOWN AND ACROSS - 5 Letter Words (Continued)

Q	R	S	T	U	V	W	Y
quack	rabbi	saber	tabby	ulcer	valet	wagon	yacht
quail	rabid	sable	table	ultra	valid	waist	yearn
quake	racer	sabot	taboo	umber	value	waken	yeast
qualm	radar	sabre	tacky	uncle	valve	washy	yield
quart	radio	salad	taffy	under	vapor	waste	yodle
quash	rainy	sales	taint	undid	vaunt	watch	young
quasi	raise	salon	tally	unfit	velum	water	youth
queen	rajah	salty	tango	unite	venom	waver	yucca
queer	rally	salve	taper	untie	venue	weary	
quell	ranch	sandy	tapir	until	verge	weave	
query	range	sauce	tarry	upper	verse	wedge	
quest	rangy	saucy	taste	usage	vicar	weedy	
queue	ratan	savor	tasty	usher	video	weigh	
quick	ratio	scald	taunt	usury	vigil	weird	
quiet	ravel	scale	taupe	utter	villa	welch	
quill	raven	scalp	tawny		vinyl	whale	
quilt	rayon	scamp	teach		viola	wharf	
quirk	reach	scant	tease		viper	wheel	
quoit	react	scare	teeth		virus	whelp	
quote	rebel	scarf	tempt		visit	where	

Z
zebra
ziffy
zloty

DOWN & ACROSS

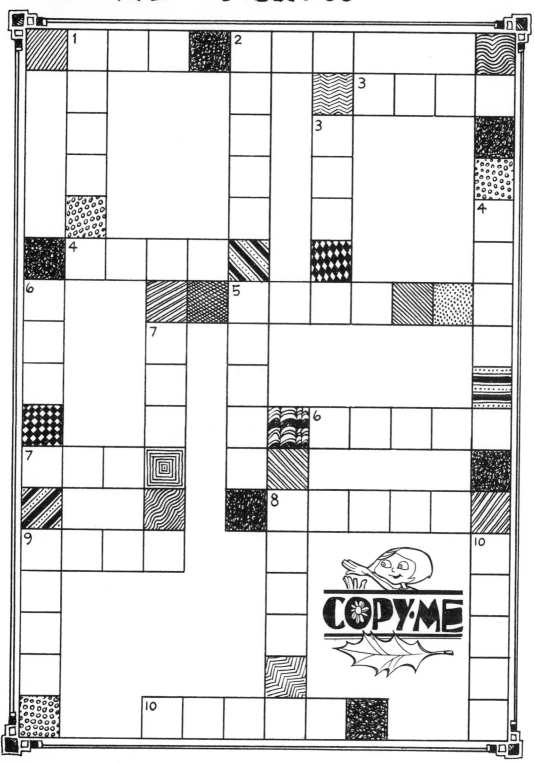

"Choose the words for this activity from the lists in the Appendix. To facilitate playing and delivery, write your chosen words here. The number of blanks indicate the number of letters in the word."

LEADER'S WORD LIST

PATTERNS SHOW WORDS THAT SHARE THE SAME FIRST LETTER

DOWN   ACROSS

1 _ _ _ _ _   1 _ _ _ _

2 _ _ _ _ _ _   2 _ _ _ _ _

3 _ _ _ _ _   3 _ _ _ _ _

4 _ _ _ _ _ _ _   4 _ _ _ _ _ _

5 _ _ _ _ _ _   5 _ _ _ _ _ _ _

6 _ _ _ _ _   6 _ _ _ _ _

7 _ _ _ _ _   7 _ _ _ _ _

8 _ _ _ _ _ _ _   8 _ _ _ _ _ _ _

9 _ _ _ _ _   9 _ _ _ _ _ _

10 _ _ _ _ _   10 _ _ _ _ _ _

YOUR NUMBER'S UP

I. **OBJECTIVE:** For the players to quickly arrange themselves in the order given.

II. **VALUE:** To increase visual perception and the ability to correctly arrange persons in a given amount of space. Practice in reading numbers.

III. **LEVEL:** Beginning through advanced. (Children to adults)

IV. **MODE:** Numbers. (Signed)

V. **MATERIALS NEEDED:**

    1. Thinking caps.

VI. **TO PLAY:**

    1. Give each player a number from 1 to 10. Each player holds his hand in the number assigned to him.

    2. The teacher (or leader) signs a number, large or small, and the players whose numbers are included must jump up and arrange themselves, <u>without</u> <u>communicating</u>, in the proper order.

    3. Play continues in like manner with numbers being called in rapid succession.

NOTE: To increase difficulty:

    1. For beginners use numbers only 0 to 9.

    2. Next use 10 to 19.

    3. Next use 20 to 99.

    4. Next use the hundreds (e.g. 249, 621, 763, etc.)

    5. Next use the thousands (e.g. 1,364, 7,892, etc.)

    6. Continue increasing.

1. Prepare players as above but instead of signing numbers, sign simple mathematical problems:

   e.g.
   $$2 + 7 = \underline{\hspace{1cm}}.$$
   $$10 - 2 = \underline{\hspace{1cm}}.$$
   $$9 \div 3 = \underline{\hspace{1cm}}.$$
   $$3 \times 2 = \underline{\hspace{1cm}}. \qquad \text{etc.}$$

2. Players must quickly figure out the problem and then those players whose numbers are included in the answer respond as in regular game.

3. The level of difficulty can be increased simply by increasing the difficulty of the problems but one must be careful not to overtax the players' mental math ability.

VARIATION II:

1. Prepare players as above.

2. The teacher or leader delivers numbers in the way they occur in our society - but using signed numbers. This provides opportunity for reading real number patterns that have natural pauses in them.

   e.g. a. social security numbers

   103-89-7465

   b. telephone numbers

   473-6210

   c. zip codes

   21813

   d. area codes

   201

   e. addresses (usually range from 2 to 5 numbers)

   21 or 643 or 3594 or 17430

GESTURE
or
PANTOMIME

EXPRESSION
or
MOVEMENT
GAMES

I. <u>OBJECTIVE</u>: To successfully portray an animal using gesture or mime.

II. <u>VALUE</u>: To increase visual awarenss of details and the ability to communicate these without the use of speech or sign.

III. <u>LEVEL</u>: Beginning through advanced. (Children to adults)

IV. <u>MODE</u>: Gesture or mime.

V. <u>MATERIALS NEEDED</u>:

    1. 3x5 cards with names of animals printed on them (see Appendix) <u>or</u> pictures of the animals may be used for younger children.

VI. <u>TO PLAY</u>:

    1. Each player in turn chooses a card.

    2. The player first shows the facial expression of the animal.

    3. Then he makes gestures to show the legs of the animals.

    4. And lastly the player moves the legs.

    5. Other players may now guess which animal is being portrayed.

<u>NOTE</u>: Sometimes facial expression will be all that is needed. Other times it may be necessary to add size, color and additional characteristics before it is guessed.

APPENDIX: ANIMAL ANTICS

ZOO	FARM	DOMESTIC
bear	duck	cat
elephant	chicken	dog
fox	horse	mouse
wolf	turkey	hamster
zebra	sheep	
lion	cow	
tiger	pig	WILD
giraffe	goat	
kangaroo	rabbit	bat
monkey		deer
camel		squirrel
seal		beaver

I. <u>OBJECTIVE</u>: For the group to complete a series of activities in the correct order.

II. <u>VALUE</u>: To increase the ability to communicate ideas without the use of speech, sign or fingerspelling and also to read that same type of communication from others.

III. <u>LEVEL</u>: Beginning to advanced. (Children to adults)

IV. <u>MODE</u>: Gesture and pantomime.

V. <u>MATERIALS NEEDED</u>:

    1. Directions for Appendix.

    2. 3x5 cards.

VI. <u>TO PLAY</u>:

    1. Using a set of directions in the Appendix, write one direction per card <u>or</u> create your own set.

    2. Mix up the cards and distribute one per player. Players must not show their cards to other players. (If you have 10 players - you must use only the <u>first</u> 10 cards of the sequence or the sequence will not work out properly.

    3. The person who has the first card in the set, gets up and does whatever the card instructs.

    4. The second activity is contingent on the first so the action will continue to move as long as each player is successful in communicating his directions.

    5. If a player fails to communicate correctly the action will come to a grinding halt. In that case, each player must reexamine his directions and the game starts back at player #1 again. This will continue until the entire sequence has been played through without error.

    6. For advanced students, when the sequence is completed, go back and discuss each individual activity for strengths and weaknesses.

APPENDIX: - CONTINGENCY GAME

Copy each direction on a separate 3x5 card.

e.g. A - (Related story with definite end).

1. You are first. Please take your seat in the orchestra and tune your flute. (stay there)

2. After someone has tuned his flute, you join him and tune your violin. (stay there)

3. After the violin is tuned, join the group and tune your cello. (You need a chair!) (stay there)

4. After the cello is tuned, please join the group and tune your percussion instruments (drums, cymbals, triangle, etc.) (stay there)

5. After the percussion instruments are tuned, join the group and tune your slide trombone.

6. After the slide trombone is tuned, join the group and tune your harp. (You need a chair!) (stay there)

7. You are the conductor. After the harp is tuned, take the podium, tap with your baton for attention and lead the orchestra in the National Anthem.

e.g. B - (Unrelated items - with no real ending)

1. You are first. Take a seat on a bus and read the paper. (Then return to your seat)

2. After the person on the bus has read the paper, you stand up, stretch and yawn. (Then sit down)

3. After the sleepy person sits down go get a drink from the fountain in the corner of the room. (Then return to your seat)

4. After someone gets a drink, answer the phone on the teachers desk and write down a message. (Then return to your seat)

5. After someone has taken a phone message, snuff out the candles on the dining room table and clean up the crumbs. (Return to your seat)

6. When someone has cleaned off the table you .....etc.

7. Continue in like manner. There are infinite possibilities. You are limited only by your imagination.

118

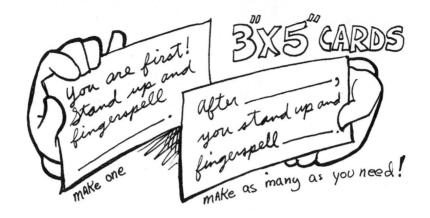

APPENDIX: - CONTINGENCY GAME (Continued)

e.g. C - (Fingerspelling - Unrelated)

    1. You are first. Stand up and fingerspell <u>happy</u>.

    2. After <u>happy</u> you stand up an fingerspell <u>book</u>.

    3. After <u>book</u> you stand up and fingerspell <u>chair</u>.

    etc.

e.g. D - (Signs - Unrelated)

    1. You are first. Stand up and sign <u>dress</u>.

    2. After <u>dress</u> you stand up and sign <u>shoe</u>.

    3. After <u>shoe</u> you stand up and sign <u>coat</u>.

    etc.

NOTE: 1. To increase difficulty of e.g. C & D, use 2 or more fingerspelled words or signs.

2. To make preparation of e.g. C & D easier, type out the following format and duplicate the number needed. Fill in the blanks by hand. Make sure you make one card read: <u>You</u> <u>are</u> <u>first</u>.

I. OBJECTIVE: To correctly imitate the actions of the teacher or leader.

II. VALUE: To provide hand and eye training using simple motions that are not formal signs. These can be used for beginner's warm-up exercises.

III. LEVEL: Beginning. (Preparation for formal signs). (Children or beginning adults) (Adults will willingly participate in this without feeling childish only if the teacher participates also and the purpose is thoroughly explained).

IV. MODE: Imitative movement.

V. MATERIALS NEEDED:

1. Finger plays from Appendix A or (Appendix B).

VI. TO PLAY:

1. Teacher selects finger play(s) from Appendix A.

2. Read it aloud without actions to the group. (To gain familiarity with the words).

3. Read it again with motions (to see how the action fits the words).

4. Read it a third time with students joining in on the motions. (It isn't necessary for students to repeat the words). Finger plays may need to be repeated several times before smoothness and fluidity are attained.

NOTE: The finger plays in the appendix are old and familiar ones. Adult students may use or have used others with their own children that they would like to share as well.

While this task may seem overly simple it is much more difficult for adults than children. Because there is usually only one gesture per line or concept, it allows time for the teacher to observe carefully that the hand configurations of group members are exact imitations of the leader. This is extremely important as ability to perceive correctly and imitate accurately is basic to learning a language whose modality is movement.

12

THE FAMILY

This is my father.
   (hold up your thumb.)
This is my mother.
   (hold up your pointing finger.)
This is my brother tall.
   (hold up your middle finger.)
This is my sister.
   (hold up your ring finger.)
This is the baby.
   (hold up your little finger.)
Oh! How we love them all!
   (clasp your hands together.)

GRANDMA'S SPECTACLES

Here are Grandma's spectacles.
   (make circles with your fingers and
   hold them over your eyes to look
   like spectacles.)
And here is Grandma's hat;
   (put both hands on your head and
   make a pointed hat.)
And here's the way she folds her hands
   (fold your hands and place them in
   your lap.)
And puts them in her lap.

Here are Grandpa's spectacles,
   (with your fingers, make larger
   spectacles for Grandpa.)
And here is Grandpa's hat;
   (make a larger pointed hat for Grandpa.)
And here's the way he folds his arms
   (fold your arms across your chest.)
\nd sits like that.

BABY SEEDS

In a milkweed cradle,
Snug and warm,
Baby seeds are hiding,
Safe from harm.
   (Cup your two hands together.)

Open wide the cradle.
   (let your hands open slowly.)
Hold it high.
   (stretch your arms high.)
Come, Mr. Wind,
Help them fly!
   (make fly-away motions to show the
   seeds sailing away in the wind.)

ALL FOR BABY

Here is a ball for Baby,
   (cup your hands to make a ball.)
Big and soft and round!
Here is Baby's hammer -
   (pound your fists together.)
O, how he can pound!
Here is Baby's music -
   (clap your hands.)
Clapping, clapping so!
Here are Baby's soldiers,
   (hold up all ten fingers.)
Standing in a row.

Here's the Baby's trumpet,
   (hold your two fists to your mouth
   and pretend you are blowing a horn.)
Toot-too-toot! too-too!
Here's the way that Baby
   (cover your eyes with your hands and
   peek through your fingers.)
Plays at "Peep-a-boo!"
Here's a big umbrella -
   (make an umbrella with your hands
   over your head.)
Keep the Baby dry!
Here's the Baby's cradle -
   (cup your hands to make a cradle
   and rock it to and fro.)
Rock-a-baby-by!

ROW, ROW, ROW

Row, row, row your boat
   (rowing motion, both hands.)
Gently down the stream.
   (forward waving motion, one hand.)
Merrily, merrily, merrily, merrily,
   (clap hands.)
Life is but a dream.
   (sleep.)

APPENDIX:A FINGER PLAYS (Continued)

WHERE IS THUMBKIN?

(Make your hands into fists. Hide them
behind your back.)

Where is Thumbkin?
Where is Thumbkin?
Here I am!
   (bring out one fist and show one thumb.)
Here I am!
   (bring out the other fist and show the
   other thumb.)
How are you this morning?
   (wiggle the first thumb.)
Very well, I thank you.
   (wiggle the other thumb.)
Run away!
Run away!
   (hide your hands behind your back again.)
   (use the same motions to show each of
   your other fingers.)

Where is Pointer?
Where is Pointer?
Here I am!
Here I am!
How are you this morning?
Very well, I thank you.
Run away!
Run away!

Where is Middleman?
Where is Middleman?
Here I am!
Here I am!
How are you this morning?
Very well, I thank you.
Run away!
Run away!

Where is Ringman?
Where is Ringman?
Here I am!
Here I am!
How are you this morning?
Very well, I thank you.
Run away!
Run away!

Where is Pinky?
Where is Pinky?
Here I am!
Here I am!
How are you this morning?
Very well, I thank you.
Run away!
Run away!

THIS IS THE CIRCLE THAT IS MY HEAD

This is the circle that is my head.
   (raise your arms above your head
   to make a big circle for the sun.)
This is my mouth with which words
   are said.
   (point to your mouth.)
These are my eyes with which I see.
   (point to your eyes.)
This is my nose that's a part of me.
   (point to your nose.)
This is the hair that grows on my
   head.
   (point to your hair.)
This is my hat all pretty and red.
   (put your hands on your head and
   make a pointed hat.)
This is the feather so bright and
   gay.
   (use your pointing finger to make
   a feather.)
Now I'm all ready for school today.

RIGHT HAND, LEFT HAND

(Each line of this rhyme will tell
you what to do with your hands.)

This is my right hand.
I'll raise it up high.
This is my left hand.
I'll touch the sky.
Right hand, left hand,
Roll them around.
Left hand, right hand,
Pound, pound, pound!

ONCE I SAW A BUNNY

Once I saw a bunny
　(make a bunny's head with your right
　hand in the letter "V".)
And a green cabbage head.
　(make a cabbage head with your left
　fist.)
"I think I'll have some cabbage,"
The little bunny said.
　(make the bunny hop to the cabbage.)
So he nibbled and he nibbled,
　(make nibbling motions with the fin-
　gers of your right hand.)
Then he pricked his ears to say,
　(straighten up the two fingers that
　are the bunny's ears.)
"Now I think it's time
I should be hopping on my way."
　(let the bunny hop away.)

WHITE SWAN

Come, pretty white swan,
Swimming over the lake,
　(move your hands to make the swan
　swim along.)
I've brought you some bread crumbs
And small bits of cake.
　(make the swan's head dip down into
　the water and up again, as it eats.)
Take care, pretty swan!
Swim away! Swim away!
　(move your arm quickly to make the
　swan swim away.)
There's a great hungry crocodile
Coming this way.
　(make crocodile motions, with jaws
　opening and closing.)
Snip, snap! go his jaws.
He is frightful to see.
But he'll never catch you!
　(point outward.)
And he'll never catch me!
　(point to yourself.)

TEN LITTLE INDIANS

(hold up a finger as you count each
　little Indian.)

One little, two little, three little
　　Indians,
Four little, five little, six little
　　Indians,
Seven little, eight little, nine little
　　Indians,
Ten little Indian boys.

(fold down a finger as you count each
　little Indian.)

Ten little, nine little, eight little
　　Indians,
Seven little, six little, five little
　　Indians,
Four little, three little, two little
　　Indians,
One little Indian boy.

BIRDS ON POLES

Two telegraph poles:
　(holding up both hands with index
　fingers erect.)
Across them a wire is strung.
　(Ends of middle fingers touching)
Two little birds hopped on
　(thumbs extending above wire made
　by middle fingers)
And swung and swung and swung.
　(swing hands back and forth.)

APPENDIX: A FINGER PLAYS

LITTLE PIG

This little pig went to market;
This little pig stayed at home;
This little pig had roast beef;
This little pig had none;
This little pig said
    "Wee, wee, wee!"
All the way home.

HERE IS THE CHURCH

Here is the church,
And here is the steeple.
Open the door,
And here are the people.

FIVE LITTLE PIGS

This little pig
Danced a merry, merry jig;
  (point to your thumb)

This little pig
Ate candy;
  (point to your pointing finger)

This little pig
Wore a blue and yellow wig;
  (point to your middle finger)

This little pig
Was a dandy;
  (point to your ring finger)

This little pig
Never grew to be big--
So they called him Tiny Little Andy.
  (point to your little finger)

THE COUNTING LESSON

THE BEEHIVE
  (make a fist with your right hand.
  This is a beehive. Bring out a
  finger as you count each bee.
  Begin with your thumb.)
HERE IS THE BEEHIVE. Where are the
    bees?
Hidden away where nobody sees.
Soon they come creeping out of the
    hive --
One!-two!-three!four!five!

THE ANT-HILL

(Make a fist with your left hand.
This is an ant hill. Bring out a
finger as you count each bee. Begin
with your thumb.)

Once I saw an ant-hill
With no ants about;
So I said, "Dear little ants,
Won't you please come out?"

Then as if the little ants
Had heard my call--
One two!three!four! five came out!
And that was all!

HANDS ON SHOULDERS

(The rhyme will help you know what
to do.)

Hands on shoulders, hands on knees,
Hands behind you, if you please;
Touch your shoulders, now your nose,
Now your hair and now your toes;

Hands up high in the air,
Down at your sides; now touch your hair;
Hands up high as before,
Now clap your hands, one, two, three,
    four.

EENSY, WEENSY SPIDER

Eensy, weensy spider
Climbed up the water spout.
   (put the tip of your right pointing
   finger against the tip of your left
   thumb. Now, keeping your fingertips
   together, twist your hands around
   and put the tip of your left pointing finger against the tip of your
   right thumb. Twist again, putting
   your right finger against your left
   thumb. Keep doing this to make the
   spider climb.)
Down came the rain
   (make a sweeping motion downward with
   both hands to show rain falling.)
And washed the spider out.
Out came the sun
   (Make a circle over your head with
   your arms for the sun.)
And dried up all the rain.
So the eensy, weensy spider
   (make the spider climb up again.)
Climbed up the spout again.

THIS OLD MAN

This old man, he played one,
   (hold up one finger.)
He played knick-knack on his thumb.
   (tap your thumbs together.)
Knick-knack, paddy-whack, give the dog
      a bone,
   (clap your hands on your knees; clap
   your hands together; then hold out
   one hand as if you were giving a
   bone to a dog.)
This old man came rolling home.
   (make a rolling motion with your
   hands.)
This old man, he played two,
   (hold up two fingers.)
He played knick-knack on his shoe.

   (touch your shoe, repeat lines 3
   and 4 above.)

This old man, he played three,
   (hold up three fingers.)
He played knick-knack on his knee.
   (touch your knee. Repeat lines
   3 and 4.)

This old man, he played four,
   (hold up four fingers.)
He played knick-knack on the floor.
   (touch the floor. Repeat lines
   3 and 4.)

This old man, he played five,
   (hold up five fingers.)
He played knick-knack on his drive.
   (touch the floor. Repeat lines
   3 and 4.)

This old man, he played six,
   (hold up six fingers.)
He played knick-knack on his sticks.
   (tap your pointing fingers together. Repeat lines 3 and 4.)

This old man, he played seven,
   (hold up seven fingers.)
He played knick-knack along to Devon.
   (point away from you. Repeat lines
   3 and 4.)

This old man, he played eight,
   (hold up eight fingers.)
He played knick-knack on his pate,
   (touch your head. Repeat lines
   3 and 4.)

This old man, he played nine,
   (hold up nine fingers.)
He played knick-knack on his spine.
   (touch your back. Repeat lines
   3 and 4.)

This old man, he played ten,
   (hold up ten fingers.)
He played knick-knack now and then.
   (clap your hands. Repeat lines
   3 and 4.)

LITTLE BOY BLUE

Little boy blue,
Come blow your horn, (beckon and blow horn.)
The sheep's in the meadow,
  (point to the right.)
The cow's in the corn!
  (point to the left.)
Where is the boy who looks after the
  sheep?
  (raise arms questioningly.)
He's under the haystack fast asleep.
  (sleep)

Run through the meadow,
  (running motion, either hands
  or feet.)
Swim in the sea,
  (swimming motion, hands and
  arms.)
Slide down a mountain,
  (sliding motion with hand.)
Climb up a tree!
  (climbing motion, hands move
  upward above each other.)

AROUND AND ABOUT

Around and about,
Around and about,
  (circular motion of index finger.)
Over and under
  (swooping over-and-under motions with
  hand.)
And in and out.
  (wriggling in-and-out motions with
  hand.)

DIG A LITTLE HOLE

Dig a little hole,
  (dig)
Plant a little seed,
  (drop seed.)
Pour a little water,
  (pour)
Pull a little weed.
  (pull up and throw away.)

Chase a little bug -
  (chasing motions with hands.)
Heigh-ho, there he goes!
  (shade eyes.)
Give a little sunshine,
  (cup hands, lift to the sun.)
Grow a little rose.
  (smell flower, eyes closed,
  smiling.)

ONE, TWO, BUCKLE MY SHOE

One, two, buckle my shoe,
  (buckle shoe.)
Three, four, knock at the door,
  (knock)
Five, six, pick up sticks,
  (pick up sticks.)
Seven, eight, lay them straight,
  (lay sticks in a row.)
Nine, ten - a big, fat hen!
  (pull out chest, pull in chin,
  hold arms out and curved at
  sides for wings.)

MY GARDEN

This is the way I plant my garden,
Digging, digging in the ground.
  (pretend you are digging.)
The sun shines warm and bright above it.
  (make a big circle with your arms for
  the sun.)
Gently the rain comes falling down.
  (let your fingers flutter like falling
  rain.)

This is the way the small seeds open.
  (let your closed fists open slowly.)
Slowly the shoots begin to grow.
  (push the fingers of both hands upward.)
These are my pretty garden flowers.
  (hold up all ten fingers to show your
  flowers.)
Standing, standing in a row.

I AM A TAILOR

I am tailor
Making clothes.
  (pretend you are sewing.)
Stitch, stitch, stitch
My needle goes.

I am a cobbler
Mending a shoe.
  (pretend you are hammering.)
Rap, tap, tap,
And it's just like new.

I am a policeman.
I stand just so,
  (stand straight and tall.)
Telling cars to stop,
  (hold out your left arm to stop cars.)
Telling cars to go.
  (motion with your right arm for cars
  to move ahead.)

SOLDIERS

Five little soldiers
Standing in a row;
  (hold up five fingers for the
  soldiers.)
Three stood straight,
And two stood so!
  (hold three fingers straight.
  let two bend over.)

Along came the captain,
  (move the pointing finger of
  your other hand in front of
  the five little soldiers.)
And what do you think?
  (Quickly straighten up all
  five fingers.)
They all stood straight
As quick as a wink!

TEN LITTLE FIREMEN

Ten little firemen
Sleeping in a row;
  (hold out your hands with fingers curled to make the sleeping firemen.)
Ding, dong goes the bell,
  (pull down on the bell cord-)
And down the pole they go.
  (with your fists together, make
  your hands slide down the pole.)
Off on the engine,
Oh, oh, oh,
  (pretend you are steering a fire
  engine very fast.)
Using the big hose,
So, so, so!
  (make a nozzle with your fist
  and pretend to use a big fire
  hose.)
When all the fire's out,
Home so-o slow.
  (steer the engine very slowly.)
Back to bed,
All in a row.
  (curl all ten fingers again to
  show the firemen asleep.)

IF

If I were a horse -
I'd neigh, of course!
  (fingers for ears. Neigh the word
   "neigh".)
If I were a bug,
  (cup hands.)
I'd curl up in a rug!
  (hug self.)
If I were a bear,
  (hold hands like paws.)
I'd comb my hair!
  (comb hair all over body.)
If I were a pig,
  (puff cheeks.)
I'd ride in a gig!
  (hold reins, jog.)
If I were a hen,
  (flap arms.)
I'd scratch in my pen.
  (scratch ground.)
If I were a lynx,
  (touch "whiskers".)
I'd sit like a sphinx!
  (hold arms stiffly forward at waist
   height, hold head stiff and close
   eyes.)
If I were a snail,
I'd crawl on the trail!
  (raise arms in roof shape. Crawling
   motion of fingers.)
But if I were a gnu --
  (fingers for horns.)
I'd have nothing to do!
  (raise hands. Shrug shoulders.)

TWO LITTLE DICKYBIRDS

Two little dickybirds
Sitting on a wall-
  (rest index fingers on table.)
One named Peter,
  (lift and replace right finger.)
One named Paul.
  (lift and replace left finger.)
Fly away, Peter.
  ("fly" right index finger over
   shoulder and change to middle
   finger.)
Fly away, Paul.
  (Repeat with left hand.)
Come back, Peter!
  ("fly" right hand over shoulder,
   change back to index finger.)
Come back, Paul!
  (repeat with left hand.)

THREE BLIND MICE

Three blind mice,
  (cover eyes.)
Three blind mice,
See how they run,
  (shade eyes)
See how they run.

They all ran after the farmer's wife.
  (running motions with fingers.)
She cut off their tails with a carving
      knife.
  (swooping, cutting motion.)
Did you ever see such a sight in your
      life
  (raise hands.)
As three blind mice!
  (cover eyes.)

APPENDIX: B FINGER PLAYS (Continued)

Additional Resources for Finger Play activities:

1. Fun with Action Rhymes (Rhythmic Activities for Younger Children) by Marie Frost, illustrated by Helen Endres, 1967 - David C. Cook Publishing Co., Elgin, Illinois 60120.

2. Finger Fun (Finger Plays for Kindergarten and Primary with Songs and Poems.) Jingles by Marguerite Gode, illustrated by Bertha Kerr, 1962 - Hayes School Publishing Co., Inc., Wilkinsburg, Pennsylvania.

3. Follow the Leader (A Book of Action Rhymes for Young Children), 1960, David C. Cook Publishing Co., Elgin, Illinois 60120.

HUMAN SCULPTURE

I.   OBJECTIVE: To create "pictures" by arranging a person or several per-
     sons to become like an object.

II. VALUE: To become aware of the configuration of objects in the space
     around us and be able to conform the body to match those config-
     urations.

III. LEVEL: Beginning through advanced. (Children to adults)

IV. MODE: Frozen positions.

V.   MATERIALS NEEDED: 3x5 cards with items from Appendix printed on them.

VI. TO PLAY:

1. Arrange players in small group(s) (3 to 6 per group).

2. Choose a leader for each group.

3. Choose a "picture" to create from list in Appendix and tell
    the group(s).

4. Instruct the leader(s) to arrange the group members into a human
    sculpture. There should be no talking or signing which would in-
    terfere with the concentration on line and form. The leader must
    be the one who visualizes the "pictures" and conceives how to re-
    produce it. He also must manipulate the hands, arms, legs, body
    etc. of the group members without any verbal instruction.

NOTE: One leader per group is crucial in this activity. If each mem-
       ber tries to create his/her own idea simultaneously - only
       chaos will result.

       Properly done this activity has infinite possibilities and is
       fascinating to watch.

131

<u>VARIATION I</u>: (simpler)

    1. Instead of using the 3x5 cards with words, cut out <u>pictures of</u> <u>people</u> in varied poses and paste them on cards.

    2. Give a picture to each group who will arrange themselves to match the picture. Particular attention should be paid to details such as fingers, angles of head, feet and facial expressions.

APPENDIX: HUMAN SCULPTURE

table and chair
a water fountain
New York City skyline
a TV set
flowers along a fence
candle

a furniture arrangement
books on a shelf
garden sculpture
sports items
    (goalpost - basketball hoop - tennis
    net - bowling pins, etc.)

HUMAN TIC TAC TOE

I. <u>OBJECTIVE</u>: To get three of a kind in a row, diagonally, horizontally, or vertically.

II. <u>VALUE</u>: 1. To increase visual awareness.
2. To become conscious of use of space.

III. <u>LEVEL</u>: Beginning through advanced.

IV. <u>MODE</u>: Silent movement only.

V. <u>MATERIALS NEEDED</u>:

1. 9 chairs.

2. Thinking caps.

VI. <u>TO PLAY</u>:

1. Divide the group into two (2) teams of 6 or 7 players each. Division by male and female players is the simplest way but if not enough males or females are present then:

   a. color code the 2 teams with colored squares of paper pinned on them, e.g. red and blue.

   b. symbol code the 2 teams with papers marked X and 0 pinned on them.

   c. have members of one team hold hand in the letter X and the other team holds the letter 0.

2. Arrange the 9 chairs in this fashion:

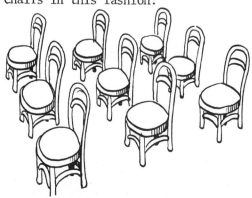

3. The first person from Team A sits down in the chair of his/her choice.

4. Next, the first person from Team B sits down in the chair of his/her choice.

5. Steps 3 and 4 are repeated until one of the teams has succeeded in making Tic Tac Toe.

6. The point goes to the succeeding team. If no Tic Tac Toe can be made the point is lost.

7. Teams should stay in the same line order as the play continually moves up.

8. If any individual tells a player where to sit his/her team loses a point.

9. Multiple games can be played simultaneously.

I. OBJECTIVE: To pantomime an activity clearly enough that it is understood.

II. VALUE: To show the part that everyday activities play in communication and increase visual awareness.

III. MODE: Gesture and pantomime.

IV. LEVEL: Beginning through advanced. (Children to adults) (Difficulty of activity adjusted to age level)

V. MATERIALS NEEDED:

1. Choose an invisible game from the appendix or create your own.

2. Select players.

3. Players "play" the game without props, paying close attention to the details of the game. The details cover a wide range - hand-shapes and movement, body involvement, facial expression.

4. When the game is over the spectators can analyze and critique the overall performance as well as individual "moves" within the game for strengths and weaknesses. What made one action more convincing than another? etc.

NOTE: With persons unfamiliar with activities of this nature, it would be well to play a short section of each game with the appropriate props or materials. This gives the players an opportunity to access the space involved as well as go through the real action of the game.

APPENDIX: THE INVISIBLE GAME

     jump rope (3 or more players)
lasso game (1 "cowboy" lassoes one or more "horses").
tug-o-war (2 groups)
high-low water (3 or more players)
over the waves (3 or more players)
cat's cradle (string game - 2 players)
baseball (pitcher - batter)
basketball (2 or more players)
catch (2 or more players)
bowling (1 bowler with invisible pins or 1 bowler with "people" pins who
         sway and fall accordingly!)
ping-pong (2 players)
board games (checkers, chess, etc.)
jacks (1 or more players)
card games (solitaire, bridge, poker, rummy, etc.)
darts

I. OBJECTIVE: To use the magic wand in a variety of ways.

II. VALUE: To stretch the imagination and also to increase one's ability to perceive the basic shapes in a variety of totally different items.

III. LEVEL: Beginning through advanced. (Children to adults)

IV. MODE: Pantomime.

V. MATERIALS NEEDED:

1. Imagination (See Appendix for possibilities).

2. A magician's wand (or a long pencil).

NOTE: A magician's wand can be easily made. You'll need:

1. a 3/8" diameter piece of wooden dowel about 13" long.

2. Paint both ends white - 1 1/2" in from the end.

3. Paint the long center section black.

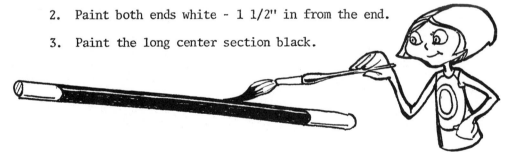

4. Abracadabra!   wand!

VI. TO PLAY:

1. Player takes the wand (or pencil) and uses it as if it were the real item. Then he passes it on to the next player who repeats the process.

2. Play continues in like manner until each player has had one turn or more.

VARIATION I:

1. Start the play as above only let players spontaneously come up and take the magic wand when they perceive a change in its use.

<u>VARIATION II</u>:   (for more advanced students who have the idea of the activity).

    1. Use an imaginary wand whose dimensions are established by describing them in pantomime.

    2. Play can proceed as in original way or in Variation I.

APPENDIX: THE MAGIC WAND

The wand can be:

a conductor's baton
a pencil
a ruler
a golf club
a cigarette
a drum stick
a violin (or cello) bow
a spoon
a telescope
a pipe
a gun
a knife
a knitting needle
a crochet hook
a baton
a pointer
a magician's wand
a spear
a yolk for carrying buckets
a cane
a paint brush

a baseball bat
a hammer
a screwdriver
an oar (for a boat)
a canoe paddle
an eyebrow pencil
a sword
a king's scepter

<u>ADD YOUR STUDENTS' IDEAS HERE</u>

_____
_____
_____
_____
_____
_____
_____
_____
_____
_____

I. <u>OBJECTIVE</u>: To correctly create instant facial expression and thereby match pairs of words that describe emotions.

II. <u>VALUE</u>: Provide practice to improve the elasticity of the face and also to learn expressions appropriate to meaning.

III. <u>LEVEL</u>: Beginning through advanced. (Children to adults)

IV. <u>MODE</u>: Facial expression.

V. <u>MATERIALS NEEDED</u>:

    1. Words chosen from Appendix A.

    2. Blank playing cards or 6x8 cards cut in half.

VI. <u>TO PLAY</u>:

    1. Write <u>each</u> word from Appendix A on 2 cards.

    2. Shuffle cards and deal out 5 per player.

    3. Player to the left of deal begins by laying down any matched pairs he holds in his hand.

    4. Next he asks any other player for a card he needs to make a pair. To do this the player must make the facial expression that matches that word and then "freeze" the face momentarily.

    5. If the player who was asked has the card he must hand it over. If he <u>thinks</u> he has the card but is unsure, he may show the card privately to the requester, who will affirm or deny its correctness.

    6. If the player does not have the card requested then the requester picks a card from the center pile.

    7. Play continues in like manner until all the cards are gone.

    8. Player with the most matches wins the game.

<u>NOTE</u>: The ability to create an expression instantaneously that is convincing and "freeze" it momentarily is not easy. It requires much analysis of facial muscles, etc. and slow practice. See Appendices B, C and D for sketches.

APPENDIX: A. MAKE-A-FACE

happiness	upset	doubt
sadness	boredom	hope
excitement	impatience	worry
fear	restlessness	embarrassment
sickness	disgust	"flabbergastion"
anger	disappointment	hate
shock	love	skepticism

APPENDIX: B MAKE-A-FACE

NEUTRAL

WORRIED

SLEEPY

HAPPY

LOVE

MAD

SAD

SUSPICIOUS

BORED

SICK

BAD SMELL

SHOCK

APPENDIX: C MAKE-A-FACE

MOUTH

PURSED

DRAWN-IN

OPEN-CORNERS DRAWN

ONE SIDE-CLOSED

LIPS PUCKERED

HALF SMILE

BOTTOM LIP POUT

DENTIST'S GRIN

EYES + BROWS

WIDE OPEN

WORRY SLANT

MAD SLANT

JOY — HAPPY

DROOP

ONE EYE SQUINT

EYES UP

BLINK ONE OR TWO

CHEEKS

PUFFED UP

ELONGATED

LIFTED UP

DRAWN-IN

NOSE

WRINKLE-UP

HEAD-TURN

142

APPENDIX: D MAKE-A-FACE

HAND POSITIONS

MEDITATION
PERPLEXED
PUZZLED

ANGUISH
EMBARRASSMENT
MORAL TORTURE

SHOCK
WHAT SHALL I DO?
YIKES!!

ARROGANT
INDIFFERENT
SNOB

ANGER
FURIOUS
IMPATIENT

LAZY
RELAXED
CARE FREE

MARIONETTE GAME

I. OBJECTIVE: To imitate the movements of a marionette and its controller.

II. VALUE: To practice control of individual parts of the body and become visually aware of the movements of others.

III. LEVEL: Intermediate through advanced. (Junior high to adult)

IV. MODE: Movement.

V. MATERIALS NEEDED:

    1. Thinking caps.

    2. Imagination.

VI. TO PLAY:

    1. Select one player to be the marionette and one to be the controller.

    2. The marionette can sit, stand or recline.

    3. The controller positions himself so the marionette can watch him/her from the corner of his/her eye.

    4. The controller begins by tying imaginary strings to the various limbs and joints of the marionette. i.e. head, shoulders, elbows, wrists, fingers, knees, ankles and feet. The controller may tie imaginary strings only to main parts, i.e. head, wrists, ankles, if he desires.

    5. The controller may move one or two strings at a time, leaving the others to just "hang down" or he may tie one up therefore keeping that limb in suspension.

6. The marionette must move his/her limbs in exactly the manner and speed that the controller pulls the strings. He must move only the limbs as directed and all others parts must hang limp.

7. The only limitation to this activity is the creativity of the controller.

NOTE: Using real marionettes first may help both the "human marionette" and the controller better understand this activity and its scope.

I. <u>OBJECTIVE</u>: To act out individual words or phrases, non-verbally and without the use of signs or fingerspelling well enough that the other player can guess the word or phrase.

II. <u>VALUE</u>: To increase the ability to think and communicate without the use of words.

III. <u>LEVEL</u>: Beginning through advanced. (All ages - adjusting level of difficulty accordingly)

IV. <u>MODE</u>: Pantomime and gestures.

V. <u>MATERIALS NEEDED</u>:

    1. A list of items (words, phrases sentences or paragraphs) to give to the students. (Appendix)

    2. Thinking caps.

VI. <u>TO PLAY</u>: METHOD A - Team Play

    1. Divide the players into two (2) teams.

    2. Team chooses an item and acts it out. A time limit may be set if desired.

    3. If the other team guesses correctly, it gets one point.

    4. Teams alternate acting out the items.

    METHOD B - Individual play without competition or scoring.

    1. One player chooses an item and acts it out. A time limit may be set.

    2. The player in the group who correctly guesses the item becomes the next player to act out.

    METHOD C

    1. Play charades with traditional items for guessing. (But <u>no</u> signs or fingerspelling is allowed)

APPENDIX: A MIME TIME

SPORTS	VEHICLES	STORES	INSTRUMENTS
football	train	drug store	violin
swimming	airline	grocery store	cello
darts	car	shoe store	harp
basketball	roller skates	clothing store	piccolo
tennis	cable car	hardware store	flute
soccer	bus	post office	slide trombone
La Crosse	truck	pet store	trumpet
Rugby	skate board	jewelry store	tuba
horseracing		bank	piano
ping-pong			clarinet

APPENDIX: B

Short Sentences

EASY

1. I'm very tired. (sleepy)
2. Are you married?
3. Are you thirsty? (hungry)
4. It's very hot outside.
5. What time is dinner?
6. That's a beautiful car.
7. I feel sick.
8. Do you have a pencil?
9. Your dress is pretty.
10. Turn down the TV.

MODERATE

1. I'll be back in 5 minutes.
2. Where is the post office?
3. How many children do you have?
4. What kind of work do you do?
5. What's your name?
6. The lecture is boring.
7. How much do you weigh?
8. I can't understand that book.
9. How many brothers and sisters do you have?
10. Can you type fast?

DIFFICULT

1. Math is my favorite subject.
2. Where were you born?
3. Your slip is showing.
4. Where did you go on vacation?
5. I'll treat you to dinner tonight.
6. I never drink whiskey.
7. What is your favorite season of the year?
8. Did you ever visit Europe?
9. I like Chinese food best of all.
10. What is your favorite sport?

I. OBJECTIVE: To mimic exactly the motions of another person.

II. VALUE: To increase awareness of movement in specific detail.

III. LEVEL: Beginning through advanced. (Children through adults)

IV. MODE: Gestures.

V. MATERIALS NEEDED:

    1. Thinking caps.

VI. TO PLAY:

    1. Select two (2) players.

    2. Choose one who will be the "mirror," and the other who will be the person looking into the mirror.

    3. Stand (or sit) players face to face.

    4. The person looking into the mirror now engages in any activity he wishes.

    5. The "mirror" must copy simultaneously all the actions of the person. Particular attention must be paid to the left and right. The person's right side will be the left side of the "mirror".

    6. Possible motions for the person.

       a. putting on make-up (women)

       b. combing, brushing hair

       c. washing

       d. brushing teeth

       e. shaving (men)

       f. checking one's appearance

g. cleaning the mirror

h. writing on mirror with soap or lipstick

i. fingerspelling or signing

j. exercising

k. singing or talking to one's self

l. making faces in mirror

NOTE: For most effective use of this exercise it is best if the <u>person</u> slows the motions considerably at first to allow the "mirror" to <u>copy</u> <u>simultaneously</u> instead of allowing a time lag.

THE PICTURE GAME

I. **OBJECTIVE:** To describe a picture so that a person can visualize it without actually seeing it.

II. **VALUE:** To train the eye to see the most important features of a picture as well as to be able to communicate the feeling in the picture.

III. **LEVEL:** Beginning through advanced. (Children to adults) Performance level may vary in accordance with age and skill in sign language.

IV. **MODE:** Gesture, sign mime and signs.

V. **MATERIALS NEEDED:**

1. Pictures of items, scenes, people, etc., cut from magazines, newspapers, etc.

VI. **TO PLAY:**

1. Players take turns describing pictures.

2. Players start with the item in the picture that is most obvious and work to complete the description. As much detail as necessary is added to make the description as vivid as possible.

e.g. This tree might be described as: tree
large
brown
bare
draw branches with index
leaf - only one, dry
          brown, orange
hang on
blow wind
soon fall maybe

NOTE: For beginners it might be more beneficial to have them repeat all previous signs each time they add one. This will give them practice in joining signs into a meaningful unit.

e.g.   tree
       tree large
       tree large brown
       tree large brown bare
       tree large brown bare (branches, etc).

I. OBJECTIVE: To establish rhythmic pattern through body movements.

II. VALUE: To increase visual awareness of body movement and be able to reproduce it. To work as part of a group.

III. LEVEL: Beginning through advanced. (Children to adults)

IV. MODE: Movement.

V. MATERIALS NEEDED: None.

VI. TO PLAY:

1. Choose one person to start a movement.

2. After the others in the group have watched and absorbed the movement, they start.

3. Eventually the entire group will be moving in perfect synchronization.

4. After synchronization has been achieved, then stop the movement, choose another leader and begin the whole process again.

NOTE: Each movement will have its own rhythm and feeling. It is important for the group just to watch until the leader has completely absorbed the rhythm he started.

VARIATION I:

1. Arrange the group of players in a circle.

2. Choose a leader who stands in the center.

3. Leader begins a movement. After he/she has absorbed it and the group has watched, then they start copying the movement.

4. When the whole group is in synchronization, the leader moves to a person in the circle (all the while continuing his movement). They change places and the new leader continues the movement.

5. Eventually the movement will change ever so slightly in the new leader and the group should follow suit and adjust their movement to be the same. (The change is an unconscious one and not premeditated.)

6. Movement continues with the leader always passing it on to a new leader.

NOTE: The final movement may have only slight resemblance to the first one.

VARIATION II:

1. Arrange group in a circle.

2. Give each player a rhythm instrument (drum, tambourine, bells, sticks, blocks, pot, oatmeal box, spoons, etc, etc. Anything that will make noise).

3. Choose a leader to start a rhythm.

4. When rhythm is established, other players join in with their instruments.

5. Simultaneity will occur for a time, then sub rhythms, and counter rhythms will start to occur, creating an "orchestral" effect.

I. <u>OBJECTIVE</u>: To be able to quickly form the external shape of the object using a rope.

II. <u>VALUE</u>: 1. To increase visual awareness for external shapes.
2. To become conscious of the use of space.

III. <u>LEVEL</u>: Beginning through advanced.

IV. <u>MODE</u>: Silent movement only.

V. <u>MATERIALS NEEDED</u>:

   1. 2 or more heavy ropes 12' or longer such as clothesline or similar weight.

   2. Thinking caps.

VI. <u>TO PLAY</u>:

   1. Divide the group into 2 or more small groups of 4 to 5 players each.

   2. Give one rope to each group.

   3. Have the players each hold onto the rope spacing themselves evenly along it.

4. The teacher calls out in voice, sign or fingerspelling, the name of some object and then the teams <u>silently</u> arrange themselves and their rope into that shape.

5. The first team to correctly make the shape, gets the point. A game can be any number of points decided upon in advance.

APPENDIX: ROPE GAME

Suggested objects for caller's use.

a ball   a snowman   a box
any number from   any letter of the   a circle, square, rec-
     0 to 9   alphabet   tangle, triangle, etc.
an apple   a flower   a ladle
a star

I. **OBJECTIVE**: To allow the "blind" person to explore the space and feel objects in his environment.

II. **VALUE**: To build trust in another person. To become aware of space and the shape of objects in that space.

III. **LEVEL**: Beginning and intermediate. (Children to adults)

IV. **MODE**: Movement.

V. **MATERIALS NEEDED**: None

VI. **TO PLAY**:

1. Arrange the players in pairs.

2. Blindfold one of each pair.

3. The other member of the pair is the "Seeing Eye Friend."

4. The "Seeing Eye Friend" then leads his blind partner around the room (or larger designated area) letting him feel all that is in his path.

5. After a set period of time has elapsed, the players change roles so the "blind" person now becomes the "Seeing Eye Friend."

WHAT'S COOKIN'?

I.   OBJECTIVE: To successfully portray specific foods using gesture or mime.

II. VALUE: To increase visual awareness of details and the ability to communicate these without the use of speech or sign.

III. LEVEL: Beginning through advanced. (Children to adults)

IV. MODE: Gesture or mime.

V.   MATERIALS NEEDED:

   1. 3x5 cards with names of foods printed on them (see Appendix)
       or pictures of food for young children.

VI. TO PLAY:

   1. Each player in turn chooses a card.

   2. The player prepares and/or cooks the food chosen by using pantomime. Pay particular attention to the peeling, cutting, mixing, stirring, cooking motions because these will vary from food to food. Also don't forget the kitchen itself-placement of cupboards, appliances, etc.

   3. Other players may then guess what the food is.

   4. Advanced students may want to analyze the various movements involved.

APPENDIX: WHAT'S COOKIN'?

Dairy	Meats	Vegetables	Fruits
cheese	steaks	green beans	peaches
eggs	hamburgers	peas	pears
butter	bacon	potatoes	apples
ice cream	fish	corn	pumpkins
cream	lobsters	cabbage	grapes
	shrimp	lettuce	bananas
		tomatoes	oranges

Miscellaneous   Baked Goods   onions   coconuts
                              beets   pineapples
nuts   cakes   spinach   strawberries
popcorn   pies   carrots
pancakes   bread   celery
waffles   cookies   salad   Beverages
soup   doughnuts
sandwiches   milk
candy   tea
pizza   coffee
                                            pop (soda)
                                            cocktails

NOTES

NOTES

NOTES